# THE PSYCHE IN THE MODERN WORLD

# United Kingdom Council for Psychotherapy Series

Recent titles in the UKCP Series
(for a full listing, please visit www.karnacbooks.com)

# THE PSYCHE IN THE MODERN WORLD

## MODERN WORLD

### Psychotherapy and Society

*Edited by*

*Tom Warnecke*

Series Consultants

Aaron Balick
Alexandra Chalfont
Steve Johnson
Martin Pollecoff
Heward Wilkinson

# KARNAC

First edition published in 2015 by
Karnac Books Ltd
118 Finchley Road
London NW3 5HT

British Library Cataloguing in Publication Data

A C.I.P. for this book is available from the British Library

ISBN-13: 978-1-78220-046-8

Typeset by V Publishing Solutions Pvt Ltd., Chennai, India

www.karnacbooks.com

# CONTENTS

# ACKNOWLEDGEMENTS

This book originated from many conversations with colleagues and lay people, with policy-makers and allied professionals. My particular gratitude belongs to my fellow authors whose ideas and contributions co-created and helped to shape this book. Of the many people who helped behind the scenes, I would like to name and thank Jessica Raby and Dr. Peter Raby for their moral support and editorial help, the members of UKCP Book Editorial Board for their encouragement and patience, Janice Brown for skilful editorial support, Ruth Martin for translating Chapter Seven, and my grandchildren for motivating me to embark on this project.

**Camila Batmanghelidjh** is a psychotherapist, children's campaigner, and founder of charities Place2Be and Kids Company. The recipient of the Centre of Social Justice's Lifetime Achievement Award and Liberty & JUSTICE's Human Rights Award, Camila has been named Ernst & Young and Coutts' Social Entrepreneur of the Year, *Third Sector Magazine*'s "Most Admired CEO", and an End Child Poverty Action Group "Champion". She is the author of *Shattered Lives: Children Living with Courage and Dignity*, and co-authored *Mind the Child: The Victoria Line*. Besides working with extraordinarily courageous children, Camila also enjoys skiing!

**Alison Bryan** MA (Oxon), Dip M Th, UKCP, initially trained as a music therapist, working at The Priory and Friern Barnet hospitals, London. She moved into psychodynamic psychotherapy while working in Hong Kong and Bangkok for eleven years, based in doctors' practices. On her return to the UK, she trained further at WPF and has had a private practice in central London since 2006 conducting long-term adult work. She published an "Autistic Group Case Study" paper and currently works at HMP Brixton for the Transitional Psychotherapy Service providing analytic psychotherapy to sex offenders.

**Alan Corbett** D Clin Sci, is a psychoanalytic psychotherapist and supervisor. He is a Trustee and Member of the Institute of Psychotherapy and Disability, Member of the Guild of Psychotherapists, and sits on the Board of Confer. He has been Clinical Director of Respond, the CARI Foundation, and ICAP, is a Consultant Psychotherapist with the Clinic for Dissociative Studies and the School of Life, and teaches on a number of psychoanalytic trainings in London and Dublin. He is the author of *Disabling Perversions: Forensic Psychotherapy with Patients with Intellectual Disabilities.*

**Claire Entwistle** BA, MA is a Chiron-trained body psychotherapist with further trainings in eating disorders and trauma, working in private practice in London since 1999. She has a special interest in the relationship between psychotherapy and the creative arts, particularly writing and singing. She has undertaken research into the question of why people become, and remain, psychotherapists. She has written a number of articles for popular and professional publications, and is working on a novel.

**Harriett Goldenberg** BA, MA, MSc, CPsychol, AdDipEx, is an existential-phenomenological psychotherapist and counselling psychologist. Canadian by birth, she trained in London, and has been in private practice for over twenty-five years, working with individuals and couples from a wide range of backgrounds, nationalities, and ethnicities. She has been teaching and facilitating at all levels of training, at the School of Psychotherapy and Counselling, Regents College, Surrey University, and the Minster Centre. Her publications include a number of journal articles and book chapters, and she co-authored, with Mary MacCallum Sullivan, *Cradling the Chrysalis: Teaching/Learning Psychotherapy* (second edition due in 2015).

**Theodor Itten** is a UKCP registered psychotherapist and psychologist MBPsS in private practice. From 1972 to 1981, he studied social science, psychology, anthropology, and philosophy in the UK and trained in psychoanalytical psychotherapy with the Philadelphia Association in London. He is a past President of the Swiss Psychotherapeutic Association and author of: *R. D. Laing: Fifty Years since The Divided Self, RAGE: Managing an Explosive Emotion, Jähzorn, Jack Lee Rosenberg, The*

*New Politics of Experience*, and *The Bitter Herbs* (with Ron Roberts). He currently lives in Sankt Gallen and Hamburg.

**Mary MacCallum Sullivan** is a psychotherapist in independent practice in Glasgow; she is Course Leader on the SIHR PGDiploma in Psychodynamic Counselling and Therapeutic Practice in Glasgow. She is a former Acting Academic Head of the School of Psychotherapy and Counselling Psychology at Regent's College, and a former Honorary Secretary of UKCP. She is Commissioning Editor for *The Psychotherapist*. She is also co-author, with Harriett Goldenberg, of *Cradling the Chrysalis: Teaching/Learning Psychotherapy* (second edition due in 2015), and has edited a number of books on a range of psychoanalytic topics.

**Michael Musalek** is a psychotherapist, a Professor of Psychiatry at the University of Vienna, and General Medical Director of the Anton Proksch Institute in Vienna. A Visiting Professor of the Sigmund Freud University in Austria and of the University of Belgrade, he has published widely and is editor of *Psychiatrie und Psychotherapie* and *Spectrum*. He is a past President of the Austrian Society for Psychiatry and Psychotherapy (ÖGPP), a member of the Executive Committee of the European Psychiatric Association (EPA), and President of the European Society of Aesthetics and Medicine (ESAM). He is co-author of *Glut und Asche—Burnout: Neue Aspekte der Diagnostik und Behandlung* and *Ars Medica: Zu einer neuen Ästhetik in der Medizin*.

**Andrew Samuels** is a Jungian analyst, university professor, author, activist, and political consultant. He is well known for his work at the interface of psychotherapy and politics. His work on sexuality, relationships, spirituality, men, and fathers has been widely appreciated. He is a former Chair of the UK Council for Psychotherapy and co-founder of Psychotherapists and Counsellors for Social Responsibility (PCSR). His many books have been translated into nineteen languages including *The Political Psyche* and *Politics on the Couch*. His most recent book is *Persons, Passions, Psychotherapy, Politics*.

**Peter Stratton** is a systemic family therapist and psychologist with broad research interests and involvement in statutory processes that affect families. His research includes development of an outcome measure for families in therapy (the SCORE project); the effects of basing training on concepts of active learning and the dialogical construction of self; the relationships of humour and creativity during psychotherapy; attributional analyses of family causal beliefs and blaming; public attitudes to terrorism by combining attributional coding with metaphor analysis. He is editor of *Human Systems*, Chair of the European FT Association Research Committee, and past Chair of the UKCP Research Faculty.

**Tom Warnecke** is a somatic-relational psychotherapist, writer, and artist with a general psychotherapy practice in London. He teaches internationally, facilitates large group events, and developed a relational-somatic approach to borderline dynamics. Previously, he also worked in community mental health services. His previous publications include a number of journal papers and book chapters, he is a co-editor of *Body, Movement and Dance in Psychotherapy*, and webcast editor for Psychotherapy Excellence (UK). He is a member of the Executive Committee of the European Association for Psychotherapy (EAP) and a past Vice Chair for the UK Council for Psychotherapy (UKCP).

# UKCP SERIES PREFACE

*Alexandra Chalfont*
Chair, UKCP Book Editorial Board

*Philippa Weitz*
Commissioning Editor, UKCP Book Editorial Board

The UK Council for Psychotherapy (UKCP), holds the national register of psychotherapists, psychotherapists qualified to work with children and young people, and psychotherapeutic counsellors; listing those practitioner members who meet exacting standards and training requirements.

As part of its commitment to the protection of the public, UKCP works to improve access to psychological therapies, to support and disseminate research, and to improve standards, and also deals with complaints against organisational as well as individual members.

Founded in the 1980s, UKCP produces publications and runs meetings and conferences to inform and consult on issues of concern to practitioners and to support continuing professional development.

Within this context, the UKCP book series was conceived to provide a resource for practitioners, with research, theory, and practice issues of the psychotherapy profession at the heart of its aims. As we develop the series, we aim to publish more books addressing issues of interest to allied professionals and the public, alongside more specialist themes.

We are both extremely proud to be associated with this series, working with the UKCP Book Editorial Board to provide publications that reflect the aims of the UKCP and the interests of its members.

# FOREWORD

*Andrew Samuels*

The contributions of psychotherapy to society beyond the alleviation of individual distress have not been much welcomed. The world did not show up for its first session. Even clinical work with individuals has been castigated as the new opium for the masses, diverting attention from social ills and fostering a false independence that scorns the virtues of communal life.

To be frank, we psychotherapists have also brought this set of frustrations upon ourselves. Too often, we are entrenched about some finer theoretical point rather than struggling for changes on the ground. The maddening rectitude of the psychotherapist allies with a mindless reductionism in which every social phenomenon is treated as if it were nothing but a psychic fragment—an unappealing pan-psychism.

Then there is the bad record of psychotherapy with regard to difference and diversity of all kinds, especially with regard to sexual minorities. Even now, when homophobia is banished, there is a tendency in the therapy world to divide people into "good gays" and "bad gays". The former ape what are claimed to be the merits of long-term heterosexual relationships and marriage. The latter are regarded as behavioural provocateurs and thoughtlessly promiscuous.

Then you have to understand how incredibly difficult it can be, unless you are relatively wealthy, to access quality psychotherapy, or your choice of modality, amongst public services in many countries. It is equally difficult for members of ethnic minorities or working-class people to train as psychotherapists. These difficulties cover a wide range of concerns including the high cost of training, the Eurocentric cast of the ideas and concepts being taught, and the bourgeois and "polite" atmosphere of many training institutes.

Last in this sin list, there is the appalling historical record of dispute and "dissing" between the various schools of psychotherapy. If our professional politics are so horrible, how on earth can we expect to be welcomed as potential contributors to political discourse and process "out there"?

I am not going to say that this book sorts all these issues out. But the content and flavour of the chapters does implicitly (and occasionally explicitly) protest against any simplistic rejection of what psychotherapy might contribute to the worldwide resistance to the cruelties and inequalities of capitalist economics. For example, we read of work with client groups that have not traditionally been part of the typical caseload of the jobbing psychotherapist—those with intellectual disabilities, or children who have no place in family, school, or society and whose behaviour, at least initially, would not make them obvious candidates for therapy.

In the book, we also read about the contribution of psychotherapy to stopping us from thinking like the establishment wants us to think. There is a quality of radical mind that, as many have noted, seems to have been present in the beginnings of the profession of psychotherapy but was subsequently lost in the pursuit of acceptance by the powerful. We see in the chapters several highly suggestive ideas about how this foundational radicalism may be recuperated.

The contemporary picture is not all rosy either. Despite powerful interventions like the one mounted by this book, we have to admit that this is not a set of problems confined to the past. Moreover, efforts to rectify things bring (as usual) their own problems. In this "social turn" or "political turn" that psychotherapy has been making since the Second World War, something may be lost in the traditional "one-person psychology" that has been swept away by relationality and theories of communication. These, it is argued, democratise therapy, making it a mutual activity—though the word "asymmetric" is usually added, and that appendage begs a multitude of questions about what the place, role, and function of the client might be. Ideas are abroad of the "active client" and even the "activist client", in which therapy is not seen any more through the prism of healer and wounded. And the famous idea(l) of the "wounded healer" deserves critique if it is used to justify incompetence, misconduct, or uncollegial acts.

"But have you wine and music still?" asks the poet of the past to the poet a thousand years hence. In all the talk of mutual recognition, rupture, and repair, and the new lexicon of relational working, what has happened to dream and fantasy, to the private and avowedly solipsistic cast of traditional psychotherapy? What place for the wholly private, poetic, mystical, and transpersonal, when the discourse is all about the "social responsibility" of the psychotherapist? Oh, yes, of course it is not a case of either/or—but there may be a conversation that needs to happen when psychotherapy apes the extraverted tendency of the culture in which it is embedded.

Despite this caveat, my personal preference is indeed for the outward perspective ("agora") that is represented in these pages, and for the way in which some of the writers use therapy thinking to challenge many psychiatric and medical orthodoxies. Why? Because the key business here is politics, and the way in which the public sphere impacts on private lives. Hence, one cannot imagine a text on the psyche in the modern world, or on psychotherapy and society, that did not shove itself in a political direction.

Reading the book has helped me achieve greater clarity about many different ways in which one can enter the evolving relationship between psychotherapy and society/politics. Of course these overlap, but listing them might be helpful.

Here are three aspects of the relationship between psychotherapy and society/politics that cluster together, for they all refer to the project of psychotherapy itself:

1. We must continue to critique and to change the practices and politics of the profession of psychotherapy. This includes questions of diversity, equality, and access. Here, too, we will find the numerous ongoing projects to make therapy culturally sensitive. If we want to see the end of silly rivalries between schools and modalities, we

should recast this, not as an intellectual or even a clinical problem, but rather as a political matter, or one of social responsibility—or even as an ethical imperative.

2. The desire to create a more diverse and more equal project of psychotherapy leads to working out the micro-politics of the therapy session itself—the power, vulnerability, and differing experiences in the therapy and in the social world of both participants. Psychotherapy both operates in a sociocultural context and is itself such a context. This is where, in my view, new discourses on, but also with, the client are much needed.

3. Being aware of the politics of the session and of the therapy relationship—not small matters—means that psychotherapists can't avoid struggling to devise new and responsible ways to engage directly with political, social, and cultural material that appears in the clinical session. The fact is that the spirit is willing but the flesh is weak. Psychotherapists yearn to work with the social dimensions of their and their client's experiences. But they lack models and concepts that would enable them to do this.

The next three in the list involve a more direct equation between psychotherapy and the political:

4. The Philosopher's Stone remains the successful and widespread application of psychotherapeutic ideas in a quest for deeper understandings of social and political processes and problems, such as the superficiality and inequity of contemporary life, or the seeming ineradicability of war and violence, or perplexing collective phenomena such as climate change denial. The problem is what we mean by "application". If we mean an interpretation from on high of what is happening done in psychotherapy's own terms, then many will find it distasteful. This is what the problem of reductionism I mentioned earlier means in practice. The great skill of psychotherapists is to be both a little outside what they are being told by the client—and also deeply in it as well. This desideratum applies also when attempting to "analyse the culture". There isn't nearly enough interdisciplinary work going on.

5. Social and political projects carried out by groups of psychotherapists remain very interesting. We have seen the formation in the mid-1990s of Psychotherapists and Counsellors for Social Responsibility, and

there have been specific issue groups concerned with nuclear weapons and climate change/sustainability. For many psychotherapists—not only psychoanalysts—the question of how to blend activism with their role and persona as professional clinicians remains an inherent difficulty.

6. Finally, there is the role of psychotherapy in developing critiques of the experience of the subject as a citizen in contemporary Western society. We lack texts on "political development" or the "political self".

The contributors to this book were not working with my list in mind! But they have covered the ground of the relationship between psychotherapy/the psyche and society/the political as comprehensively as I have ever seen it done. The writers remain "in" what they are writing about to an impressive degree and there are many novel, ingenious, and deep ideas in these pages which should interest everyone on the spectrum running from concerned citizen to psychotherapist. I was surprised by how the more global, abstract, and theoretical contributions made me think about my clinical work—and by how the clinical material and discussion turned my thoughts in a worldly direction. The book is a considerable achievement.

# INTRODUCTION

*Tom Warnecke*

A century after Freud successfully introduced psychotherapy to the world at large, it is timely to consider and discuss depth-psychology[1] and contemporary psychotherapy practice in modern-day contexts and current understanding of well-being and health. This book is conceived as an anthology of stand-alone chapters, each dedicated to themes that encompass socio-political as well as philosophical, theoretical, and clinical dimensions. The authors of this book discuss subject matters that pose challenging and often uncomfortable questions, reflecting concerns that the psychotherapy field, social and medical sciences, and policy-makers will need to address to advance well-being and well-doing in twenty-first-century societies. However, before introducing the individual chapters, I want to briefly outline some of the dynamics that commonly contextualise the provision of psychotherapy services today.

If you fracture a leg, you can expect to receive a good standard of care in most societies. Sadly, the same cannot be said if your confidence and ability to function shatter after being involved in some incident. Emotional or psychic distress may account for as much as half of all ill-health suffering in Western Europe, if we believe a World Health Organization estimate. It is also well established that most personal problems affect others, either directly or indirectly, in the family or at a workplace, but also through antisocial, sociopathic, or criminal behaviours occurring in all sections of society. Historically, policy-makers assigned lower, or even significantly less, importance to psychological or emotional well-being than to medical services, and such disparity continues in the twenty-first century, as highlighted in a landmark report by the Royal College of Psychiatrists (2013). Levels of public resources designated to support people who struggle to function within the parameters set by society vary significantly between countries. They are subject to national debates and political policies, and inevitably reflect public perceptions of benefits associated with such services but also popular political agendas within any society.

Politicians of all persuasions all too often appear to view personal unhappiness or personal autonomy with mistrust, as dissension or as threatening. The complex nature of emotions and motivation is not just challenging to science but possibly more so to political leaders and policy-makers. Psychotherapy is not a social theory but primarily concerned with the distress of individuals and their "problems of living". Peoples' struggle for vitality and meaning will usually affect others, either directly or, as the economist Richard Layard (2006) argued, via a public purse, and should thereby be considered public issues. Valuing the impact of different health conditions is a difficult undertaking but also dependent on methodology. A recent UKCP report (Fujiwara & Dolan, 2014) suggests that the public costs of depression and anxiety may be much higher than previously assessed.

Based on a meta-analysis of over fifty studies, the American Psychological Association (2012) concluded that psychotherapy is effective, helps reduce the overall need for health services, and produces long-term health improvements with fewer side-effects than medication. But there are many indications that public understanding of psychotherapy, what psychotherapy does and what it does not do, is perhaps much more limited than one might assume. Politicians and civil servants appear to be no different from the general population. Many government initiatives that bear on psychotherapy services, for example the selective psychotherapy legislation in Germany or France, appear more concerned with protectionist agendas of professional groups competing for business than with patient welfare, improving quality standards, or improving access for demographic groups commonly marginalised by or excluded from psychotherapy services.

While psychotherapy is readily available in the private sectors of high-income societies, it is much more difficult to access within public services, and this situation is often further exacerbated for demographic minorities in society. In some Western countries, efforts are made to expand access, but such initiatives will often deliver only some economy version rather than the gold standard of contemporary clinical practice. The controversial decision to introduce standardised psychological therapy treatments by Improving Access to Psychological Therapies (IAPT), the UK initiative spearheaded by Layard, is a good example. Moreover, new IAPT services frequently effected the closure of long-standing, well-respected, quality psychotherapy services. Economy psychotherapy services such as IAPT are dominated by cognitive behavioural therapies (CBT) which successfully portray their approach as a supposedly simpler, shorter, and cheaper version of psychotherapy, a brand image that ignores the fact that large parts of CBT practice consist of common and widely used psychotherapeutic interventions.

The CBT brand relies heavily on randomised control trials (RCT) to prove CBT efficacy. However, RCTs were created to test pharmacological treatments, and there are mounting concerns about their reliability as the sole (or main) evidence for psychological interventions (Loewenthal et al., 2011). Moreover, while there are a good number of RCTs that show the effectiveness of CBT—based psychotherapy for some diagnostic conditions, these trials do not compare CBT with other psychotherapy approaches and cannot provide evidence that CBT is any more or less effective than other psychotherapies. On the other hand, there is substantial research evidence for the crucial role of "common factors" (Chapter One), factors that are common to all psychotherapies. Comparative studies (Frank & Frank, 1991) and common factor research (Grencavage & Norcross, 1990) concluded that all psychotherapies generally work equally well. Research also suggests that a broad variety of modality approaches can maximise clinical outcomes since they allow clients/patients and their therapists to choose approaches that best suit their personalities and preferences.

Critics have argued that psychotherapy is "cultivating" vulnerability or dependency instead of promoting autonomy, and denounce depth-psychology's call for self-acceptance as complacency about political change in society (Furedi, 2004). While there is little evidence of cultivating dependency, there is valid concern that the embracing of vulnerability in psychotherapy is often only unilateral. The classic psychotherapy setting was originally modelled on the authoritarian family structure that dominated Western European society at the birth of the psychoanalytic movement in the late nineteenth century (Frank, 1976). Cultural values dictated that intimacies should be confined within the family but only unilaterally so: children were not supposed to keep secrets but the same did not apply to the all-powerful parents.

The hereditary asymmetry in the therapeutic relationship gives rise to the image of a disquietingly powerful psychotherapist pictured by Pilgrim (1997): a confused, vulnerable, or dysfunctional client/patient meets a therapist who is not only well functioning both socially and personally, but also skilled in therapeutic techniques designed to impact and influence others. This vulnerable person seeking psychotherapy walks into a framed context, constructed in advance by the psychotherapist. The settings for the therapeutic relationship and the range of conversations allowed or disallowed within it are largely controlled by the psychotherapist, and the relationship is neither reciprocal nor equal. Asymmetry and power dynamics are amplified further by the diplomas and certificates that attest to the competencies of the clinician, whereas clients/patients arrive with statements of incompetence or inabilities to manage some aspect of their lives.

Today's contemporary psychotherapy approaches emphasise the co-constructed nature of the therapeutic relationship. The relational paradigm, a two-person psychology approach, for instance, acknowledges that there are two people interacting mutually, if asymmetrically, in the therapeutic relationship. But such theoretical or philosophical positions nevertheless remain at the psychotherapist's discretion and the ghosts of a psychotherapist's supposed "blank screen" or "superior authority" linger on in many consulting rooms. Incidentally, such concerns provide a key argument for maintaining the highest quality standards in psychotherapy education. This could become a serious concern since economy-psychotherapy in cash-strapped public services is frequently delivered by practitioners with only minimal training or qualifications.

The second critique, self-acceptance versus political change in society, is of similar complexity. Depth-psychology has acted mostly as a socially progressive force in society—exceptions notwithstanding. Perhaps the biggest stain in the history of depth-psychology is its toxic legacy of pathologising homosexuality solely based on cultural prejudice and contrary to available evidence that same-sex attractions constitute normal variants of human sexuality (Warnecke, 2013). But there are also valid concerns that social, political, environmental, or cultural issues are commonly kept out of the consulting room in contemporary psychotherapy practice. The eminent psychoanalyst and social philosopher Horst-Eberhard Richter (1986) argued that psychoanalysis lacked "social analysis". The traditional psychoanalytic near-exclusive focus on the inner world of the individual, says Richter, is negligent when it ignores the socio-economic dynamics that contextualise the person's experience. For Richter, this recognition marked a fundamental paradigm shift and a starting point to re-orient depth-psychology from the individual to couple and family dynamics, and eventually to socio-economic psychology. Freud conceived psychoanalysis as a socio-political discipline, and depth-psychology must maintain political relevance in society to live up to this legacy, Richter (1986) observed.

Current debate about how the psychotherapy field should engage with environmental issues in the consulting room may rekindle discourse about the "political Psyche" (Samuels, 1993) and its place in psychotherapy. Political debate is intrinsically polemic and proceeds through argument and reasoning, whilst therapeutic discourse is by nature exploratory and intuitive, Staunton (2007) observes. Politics generalises whereas therapy personalises, and therapists are expected to bear the unbearable and contain rather than act or influence. Samuels (2001) challenges the notion that politics and exploration of societal issues is not the business of psychotherapy or may even be incompatible with introspection. Politics do belong on the couch, argues Samuels, but also notes the dearth of professional discourse or publications that could support their inclusion in clinical practice.

Another common critique is focused on internal conflicts and rivalries. To the casual observer, depth-psychology may appear like an intellectual zoo, riven by rivalries and seemingly irreconcilable theories. While insiders cherish and value the rich diversity of psychotherapy modalities and paradigm discourse, such plurality is difficult to comprehend by society and commonly seen as a manifestation of political and ideological infighting. The sociologist Peter Morrall is not the first to conflate the two when he observes: "Therapy enterprise has a long history of conflicts and rivalries which remain today, and choosing a type of therapy and a therapist is a lottery. Therefore, the claim is made that therapy is a deeply dysfunctional discipline" (2008,

p. 6). It would not be fair to blame Morrall for the distorted image he portrays. Depth-psychology has indeed consistently failed to present itself as the single discipline it is—a single discipline that includes a vibrant plurality of modalities within its fold.

Researchers recognise that all cohorts of patients improve on the average over time (Frank, 1972). Such findings are consistent with insights that people seek psychotherapy primarily because they are demoralised. The efficacy of all psychotherapy modalities, Frank (1991) argues, lies in their capacity to transform meaning and thereby arouse client's/patient's hopes and restore their sense of mastery in the world. We have also learned that the clinician's inter-relational presence makes therapy "work" over and above any specific technique, or types of interventions (Lambert & Barley, 2002; Loewenthal et al., 2011).

Fault-lines between society and psychotherapy may also reflect a historically uneasy relationship with the establishment. The intellectual influence of depth-psychology revolutionised the understanding of mental life and human functioning in the twentieth century, and in the process challenged not only established views in society but also prevalent power dynamics or some vested interests of the establishment on many occasions: for example, when Freud (1896) shocked Vienna's establishment at the turn of the nineteenth century with revelations that "traumatic hysteria" symptoms had their origins in premature sexual experiences and traumatic incidents of sexual abuse. Freud was forced to partially retract his assertions or risk the reputation of the fledgling psychoanalytic movement. One century and countless scandals later, Western societies are beginning to accept that such violations are not isolated incidents at all and that perpetrators commonly operate within respected and trusted institutions, the religious establishments for example, or educational, social, and media services.

Decades later, R. D. Laing (1960) not only disputed established views of psychosis but also argued that psychosis might, in part, constitute a social mechanism. Laing's views of psychosis' possible family or trauma contexts proved deeply controversial and saw affected families join forces with biologically minded psychiatrists to denounce Laing and defend the mental health policies of their time. Fifty years on from Laing's assertions, there is scant evidence to support brain disorder theories and the medicalisation of mental illnesses (BPS, 2013) which nonetheless continue to dominate mental health policies that offer little hope for a full recovery to patients.

The most serious critique of psychotherapy concerns its narrow cultural reach and appeal and the failures of depth-psychology to expand its traditional client/patient base, the articulate Western middle class, in order to engage and work with demographic groups in society that commonly struggle to access psychotherapy for various reasons. At its birth, the psychoanalytic movement blindly incorporated many Western European cultural values and normative assumptions, for example the Christian-Judaic premise that procreative sex was normative. Similarly, the concept of repression so central to psychotherapy belongs to a time when repression was the law of life in the era of nineteenth-century colonisation and white male supremacy (Hillman, 1976). While narrow or outdated cultural values and normativities cannot invalidate depth-psychology, they are increasingly getting in the way of making psychotherapy more relevant to other cultures in the world, of broadening the application of depth-psychology to include settings and client groups who cannot or will not fit into the traditional psychotherapy frame shaped to suit a Western middle-class population. Most importantly, a major review of embedded cultural assumptions might allow depth-psychology to deliver more effective advocacy for the Psyche in society.

## About the chapters

A book that includes the Psyche in its title should not dodge considering, and at least attempting to review, the concept of the Psyche. The first chapter, "Psyche and Agora—the Psyche at the crossroads of personal and societal contexts" by Tom Warnecke, explores the complex dichotomies that surround a classical Greek construct that survived two and half millennia, dualism, and the dark ages. Does the idea of the Psyche have a future in an age of quantum and neuroscience, individualism and scientism?

In the chapter "The politics of intelligence", Alan Corbett examines the concepts of intelligence and consent in the context of psychotherapy with the intellectually disabled. How we consider the thorny subjects of intelligence and consent is inevitably also a wider societal issue with a bearing on a number of professional fields, including medicine and social care. Similarly, the challenges and difficulties of supporting marginalised children go to the heart of public policies and bear on the professional activities of a range of disciplines. In the chapter

"Clinical snobbery—get me out of here!", Camila Batmanghelidjh, a well-known pioneer for cutting-edge approaches to engage with children therapeutically, describes the evolution of a therapeutic paradigm for children with complex disturbances.

Two chapters are dedicated to exploring the multi-layered relations between psychotherapy culture and concepts, on the one hand, and their impact on general culture and society, on the other. Alison Bryan's "Why aren't we educating?" explores these issues with perspectives rooted in both original and contemporary psychoanalytic paradigms. In the chapter "Psychotherapy, relationality and the Long Revolution", Mary MacCallum Sullivan and Harriett Goldenberg approach these questions informed by two-person psychology perspectives, a major contemporary paradigm shift that has affected the entire range of psychotherapy approaches.

In the twenty-first century, "evidence based" has become a fashionable term and one commonly associated with quantitative research methods such as randomised control trials. In his chapter "Human-based medicine", Michael Musalek challenges the "objectivity" assumptions inherent in this construct and lays out a comprehensive case for extending the currently ruling "evidence-based" construct towards a "human-based" paradigm, an approach based on dialogical relationships that relies on both quantitative and qualitative evidence to improve the quality and the effectiveness of medical and psychological interventions.

The chapter "Routes out of schizophrenia" by Theodor Itten, who trained at the Philadelphia Association co-founded by R. D. Laing, opens with a review of how the current understanding of mental illness evolved. The author offers and considers a number of alternative perspectives to the, in Western societies, currently dominating "degenerative brain disorder" construct that can be explored by patients and their therapists to facilitate recovery.

Claire Entwistle, in the chapter "Counting the cost", explores what motivates people to study and become psychotherapists. Utilising data from a small research project, the author considers the place of psychotherapy profession economy in psychotherapy education and in the minds of psychotherapy students, which in turn leads to some pertinent questions about modern societies in which meaningful conversation is apparently a rare commodity.

In the final chapter, "How broader research perspectives can free clients and psychotherapists to optimise their work together", Peter

Stratton sets out to unravel and investigate the complex dichotomies that impact our relationships with psychotherapy research. Unacknowledged and unresolved, Stratton argues, they form a serious obstacle to improving practitioner proficiency and advancing quality psychotherapy services.

The authors of this book would all welcome further discourse on the issues raised here, but also hope for a revival of depth-psychology as a socio-political discipline that is eager to engage in inter-disciplinary debate and, equally, in dialogue with general culture and with those who use psychotherapy services.

## Note

1. The term "depth-psychology", was coined by Eugen Bleuler to describe psychoanalytic ideas or research that take the unconscious into account and later associated with theories pioneered by Janet, James, Freud, Jung, and Hillman. In the context of this book, depth-psychology refers to explanatory psychotherapeutic concepts of the Psyche as distinct from psychotherapeutic practice or from mainstream psychology.

## References

American Psychological Association (2012). Research shows psychotherapy is effective but underutilized. http://www.apa.org/news/press/releases/2012/08/psychotherapy-effective.aspx (accessed on 3 February 2013).

British Psychological Society (2013). *DCP Position Statement on the Classification of Behaviour and Experience in Relation to Functional Psychiatric Diagnoses*. London: British Psychologial Society.

Frank, J. D. (1972). The bewildering world of psychotherapy. *Journal of Social Issues, 28*: 27–43.

Frank, J. D. (1976). Restoration of morale and behavior change. In: A. Burten (Ed.), *What Makes Behavior Change Possible?* New York: Brunner/Mazel.

Frank, J. D., & Frank, J. B. (1991). *Persuasion and Healing: A Comparative Study of Psychotherapy* (3rd edn). London: John Hopkins University Press.

Fujiwara, D., & Dolan, P. (2014). *Valuing Mental Health: How a Subjective Wellbeing Approach Can Show Just How Much It Matters*. London: UKCP.

Furedi, F. (2004). *Therapy Culture: Cultivating Vulnerability in an Uncertain Age*. London: Routledge.

Grencavage, L. M., & Norcross, J. C. (1990). Where are the commonalities among the therapeutic common factors? *Professional Psychology: Research and Practice, 21(5)*: 372–378.

Hillman, J. (1976). *Revisioning Psychology*. New York: HarperPerennial.

Lambert, M. J., & Barley, D. E. (2002). Research summary on the therapeutic relationship and psychotherapy outcome. In: J. C. Norcross (Ed.), *Psychotherapy Relationships That Work: Therapist Contributions and Responsiveness to Patients* (pp. 17–32). New York: Oxford University Press.

Layard, R. (2006). The case for psychological treatment centres. *British Medical Journal, 332*: 1030.

Loewenthal, D., Guy, A., Thomas, R., & Stephenson, S. (2011). *NICE Under Scrutiny*. London: UKCP.

Morrall, P. (2008). *The Trouble with Therapy: Sociology and Psychotherapy*. Maidenhead: Open University Press.

Pilgrim, D. (1997). *Psychotherapy and Society*. London: Sage.

Richter, H. E. (1986). *The Chance des Gewissens*. Hamburg: Hoffmann und Campe.

Royal College of Psychiatrists (2013). *Whole-Person Care: From Rhetoric to Reality*. Occasional Paper 88, London: Royal College of Psychiatrists.

Samuels, A. (1993). *The Political Psyche*. London: Routledge.

Samuels, A. (2001). *Politics on the Couch: Citizenship and the Internal Life*. London: Karnac.

Staunton, T. (2007). Therapy versus politics? *The Psychotherapist, 34*: 2.

Warnecke, T. (2013). What can psychotherapy do? Psychotherapy paradigms and sexual orientation. *International Journal of Psychotherapy, 17(2)*: 74–85.

# CHAPTER ONE

# Psyche and Agora: the Psyche at the crossroads of personal and societal contexts

*Tom Warnecke*

Psyche enjoys a prominent but peculiar presence in the public spaces of our societies through a host of words that build on the term. In common use, Psyche stands for an inner dimension and for the emotional life of a person. Perceptions of the human inner dimension vary greatly, however, depending on the discourses the Psyche is placed within: modern societies impose great dichotomies between the personal realm of the individual and their social environments.

Literature, the arts, and the entertainment media thrive on portrayals of the personal and compel with the human element. Feelings, emotions, and inner conflicts inspire artists and attract audiences. Or they enhance a story with a "human touch" when included in the margins of history books or with a current news item. Modern societies ostensibly value the human psyche, feelings, and emotions. Or do they?

For this image of societal values changes significantly when we look from up close, from the perspective of the individual. In our daily lives, we disclose feelings and inner struggles at our peril and to our shame. Emotions are feared, trivialised, or avoided. Social norms dictate that we should pull ourselves together, not make a fuss, not become hysterical, weak, or unmanly. The private and the personal, our vulnerabilities and needs, are embarrassing to us in the social space and ought to remain hidden from others and perhaps even from ourselves. Social norms require us to control or tame our feelings and inner conflicts, and we reward ourselves, above all, for not needing from others. And those who deviate, those who cannot tolerate the intolerable, commonly become stigmatised as "challenging", "disordered", or "mentally ill" by their social environment.

## The Psyche

So who or what is the Psyche? The term "Psyche" originated in ancient Greek culture and is used synonymously with soul and self. But the term has also become associated with meanings that are quite removed from the original sentiment. The Psyche is perceived by some as a "seat of the faculty of reason" but also as "mind", "ghost", or "spirit", or described as a control centre "responsible for one's thoughts and feelings". Other distortions associate the term "Psyche" with ideas of body and soul as separated or segregated from one another—reflecting Christian rejection of pluralistic conceptions, but also beliefs that the body and its senses distract us from the supernatural. In theological and philosophical discourse, the Psyche is also described as an immortal aspect of human existence (Rhode, 1925).

In classical Greek thought, the Psyche was intimately connected to the notion of life. To have a Psyche was to be alive, and all living things were seen to possess a Psyche. The Psyche stood for a principle of life, or an "animator", or an inner dimension of "soma". Greek philosophers and poets initially used the word "soma" for a corpse and referred to the body not as a unit but as an assemblage of organs. By the early sixth century BC, however, soma had become redefined as a living body (Abad, 2003). This living body is inhabited by the Psyche, but the Psyche is not associated with any bodily organs. The changing awareness of Psyche and soma coincided with new-found appreciation for the agonies of erotic desire. Eros evokes bodily states of passion, anguish, confusion, or helplessness, imbues music and poetry with expressions of sensuality, longing, and consummation, individualises our experience, and awakens the body–mind to itself. The undeniable intensity of emotional bodily experience in passionate desire and unrequited love, it seems, fostered recognition of the Psyche as the body's inner dimension.

The notion of the Psyche recognised that all living things had individuality. Western culture effectively took a quantum leap when Greek philosophers began to recognise the individual self as differentiated from its collective tribal culture. Heraclitus' distinctive use of the word "Psyche" to denote a self with infinite depth was followed a century later by Socrates' claim in 399 BC that his driving philosophical concern was to work on the Psyche. Aristotle refined the classic Greek conception further with a psychology that followed a predominantly physiological approach: the Psyche is a principle of the natural body and the Psyche's affections are "enmattered" in the body, he emphasised. Aristotle also proposed that Psyche consisted of and was defined by interdependent functional faculties and identified these as independent motion, self-nourishment, reproduction, perception, and thought.

The recognition that the Psyche is "enmattered" embraced the complexities of human existence and advanced the classic Greek conception well beyond earlier, and indeed many later, ideas that the Psyche might lead some separate existence, as a segregated, ghostly occupancy of the body, for example. The Psyche is not only an animator or inner dimension, it can only exist in perpetual exchange and connection with its natural and social environments. The conceptual and philosophical framework of the Psyche created by classic Greek thinkers is intrinsically pluralistic. It is pertinent to many disciplines, but also contains paradoxes and tensions that remain unresolved to the present day.

Modern history saw the rise of dualistic conceptions that continue to cast their shadows in today's world with ideas that mind and body are in essence or functionally separated. In the early twentieth century, the psychoanalytic movement revolutionised European understanding of human functioning. Freud, Jung, and other pioneers developed depth-psychological models of the Psyche, for example Freud's well-known structural model of the id, the ego, and the super-ego. Depth-psychology recognised the Psyche as a dynamic, self-regulating system in which conscious, unconscious, and semi-conscious processes complement each other. Modern neuroscience has built on and added to this core understanding of human functioning.

In contemporary depth-psychology, the term "Psyche" refers to the forces in an individual that influence thought, behaviour, and personality. The eminent psychologist Hillman (1976) takes the stance that the Psyche belongs to the realm of a third, middle position between the material and physical, on the one hand, and the abstract and spiritual, on the other, and yet bound to both dimensions. And the Psyche proves an elusive subject even when leaving "spirit" and other supernatural meanings aside. As soul or selfhood, the Psyche cannot be quantified and any associated phenomena, however deeply rooted in our biology, are rarely amenable to measurements and generalisations. As an object of study, the Psyche is inevitably a conversing subject. Any notion of the Psyche cannot be neutral of the observer's personal values, beliefs, and object relations, and irrespective of whether the Psyche is viewed through a philosophical, biological, psychological, or theological lens.

Research documents how the deeply personal can most powerfully impact our capacity to function. The universal experiences of shame and fear are at the root of common problems to feel joyful, real, and loved, or to experience life positively and meaning-fully (Brown, 2010). Crucially, shame and fear also create social isolation as they form formidable obstacles to feeling connected to others or to a sense of belonging to family and social networks. On the other hand, trading in personal authenticity for social or family approval is self-defeating and destructive. We need to get the balance right between socialisation and self-acceptance, Brown argues, to feel comfortable in our own skin. People who score higher on measures of authenticity have greater life satisfaction, higher self-esteem, lower depression and anxiety, fewer health complaints, and behave in more socially constructive ways (Cooper, 2013). Authenticity, self-love, and belonging are as vital to our health as nutrition or exercise and crucial to build resilience to help us cope with life's set-backs, with rejections or losses. Embracing our tenderness and vulnerability is as essential to our well-being as developing knowledge and self-determination.

The deeply personal realm informs our personal perspectives and mediates events. It is quintessentially reflective and operates by gathering and weaving threads of meaning that can hold, explore, or transport both imaginative and emotional content or communicate what Alexander's (1979) philosophy of architecture identified as the "qualities without a name" we nonetheless universally recognise. The Psyche can be seen at work in imagination and reflective capacity, in metaphor, and in works of art, in architectural design, or in theoretical physics, but is most easily discernible in moments of instantaneous connection when we suddenly feel moved by some natural event or human expression:

> "The best moments in reading", says Hector in Bennett's play *The History Boys*, "are when you come across something—a thought, a feeling, a way of looking at things—which you had thought

> special and particular to you. Now you have it, set down by someone
> else, a person you have never met, someone who is long dead. And
> it is as if a hand has come out and taken yours." (2004, p. 56)

The Psyche may freely transcend the personal but is nonetheless irre-
ducibly tied into human biology. "Without anatomy emotions do not
exist. Feelings have somatic architecture" notes Keleman (1985, p. xii).
Keleman's observation acquires further potency when taken in con-
junction with a statement by the renowned neuroscientist Damasio:
"Feelings are often ignored in accounts of consciousness. Can there be
consciousness without feelings? No. Introspectively, human experience
always involves feelings" (2010, p. 242).

## Psyche in the modern world

The term "psychology" refers to the study of the Psyche or soul, but
there is little evidence for soul studying in psychology literature. Academic psychology apparently viewed depth-psychology as a hazard
to its pursuit of scientific respectability. Paraphrasing Hillman (1964),
depth-psychology was the stone rejected by the academy-builders.
Or perhaps Frank was right when he observed that "nothing is less
appealing to the scientific mentality than uncontrolled emotion" (1971,
p. 308).

Behaviourism, once the primary science in psychology, discarded
many aspects that characterise human existence in favour of more
"objective" realities and selected factors that appeared easily amenable
to scientific study. Thoughts, emotions, motivations, or consciousness
were all considered outside the scientific domain on the basis that their
essential subjectivity rendered them inaccessible to be measured to
any objective standards. Not surprisingly, psychological research commonly ignored and missed out on many of the intricate complexities
that inform and guide human activity. Behaviourism has since developed into cognitive science, but this historic conception retains a powerful influence on contemporary psychology. Psychometric tools that
promise to profile and predict psychological behaviour patterns continue to find favour with business managers, executive coaches, and in
the human resources sector.

An alternative perspective developed in the mid-twentieth century when an emerging humanistic psychology took a more holistic

approach to human existence. The pioneering humanist thinkers Abraham Maslow and Carl Rogers argued that both psychoanalysis and behaviourism were too pessimistic by focusing either on the most tragic of emotions or failing to take into account the role of personal choice. Humanistic psychology takes the position that people are inherently good, that psychology should focus on each individual's potential, and advocates the importance of growth and self-actualisation.

Mainstream psychiatry promotes brain-based approaches to thought, emotion, and behaviour. Medical researchers look to biology and chemistry to decode human personality and behaviour, and search for biochemical treatments that could affect psychic distress and suffering. But the medicalised approach has so far only developed limited understanding of mental illness and produced little evidence for its theories (Williams, 2012). Schizophrenia, for instance, is diagnosed only by a process of exclusion. There is no laboratory test that can either prove or disprove this diagnosis, and researchers cannot say if schizophrenia has one or perhaps several aetiologies. Marcia Angell (2011), a former editor of the *New England Journal of Medicine*, questions contemporary psychiatric treatment: if currently marketed psychoactive drugs were so effective, she argues, we should expect the prevalence of mental illness to decline rather than rise.

While drugs are undoubtedly an important, or in some instances even a crucial, tool, they can rarely address the root causes of psychological or emotional distress and suffering. Treating symptoms rather than the causes provides the pharmaceutical industry with a profitable revolving-door business model but fails the patients and, equally concerning, saddles societies with steadily increasing public health budgets. Medicine is also successfully promoting views that mental distress and mental illness constitute brain-based pathologies, as the current trend to medicalise ordinary emotional responses and many normal variabilities of human life and social experience shows. Psychoactive drugs are regularly prescribed to deal with common social and psychological complaints, from exam stress to puberty, relationship problems, or bereavement (Society for Humanistic Psychology, 2012).

While dualistic "ghost in the machine" ideas have been thoroughly discredited by modern science, they nevertheless remain popular in general culture and pseudo-science. They impinge on serious engagement with any non-dualistic understanding of the Psyche and continue to resurface in various forms and guises, for example in the elevation of top-down effects of knowledge structures. In modern society, the pursuit of knowledge is mostly portrayed as an intellectual enterprise by some disembodied intellect as if "it" were afloat somewhere in space. As a consequence, academic intelligence has become the primary focus of modern education policies, whereas practical intelligence and learning are treated as inferior and secondary to abstract learning.

This is not the place to discuss the many models of consciousness, personality, or self-hood. Suffice to say that they by and large all stipulate that we can experience ourselves and our environments and that we have some capacity for becoming aware of ourselves, including some inner dimension or personal world. What is relevant in the context of this book, however, are the inseparable associations between the Psyche, our organism's personal dimension, and our emotions and affect states. Both emotions and affect states constitute unruly and messy phenomena that are rarely amenable to being tamed or controlled.

The psychoanalytic movement was born as an instrument to explore the human experience. In modern society, depth-psychology and psychotherapy emerged as the main champion and advocate for the deeply personal, for the fundamental psychological idea of personification, and for the phenomena of the imaginal Psyche (Hillman, 1976).

## Psychotherapy and the Psyche

People commonly turn to psychotherapy at times when internal and external stress factors combine and become demoralising or debilitating. Such distress may be fuelled by a lack of interpersonal or intrapersonal skills necessary to help us manage a situation. Stress or distress may also arise in situations new to us that exceed or overwhelm our abilities to function within them. Any such external stress factors may combine with, or re-inflame, pre-existing internal stress dynamics, arising from difficult, confusing, or traumatic childhood experiences, for example, that became engrained in our psychobiology. Whatever the causes, stress tolerance and the self-regulation capacities of the human species are limited, and stress or distress can easily exceed them. Consider the following scenario:

> Sally is at work. She feels calm and at ease today. Alice enters Sally's office visibly upset and in distress. Naturally, Sally is impacted by Alice's state but also able to remain calm herself. She acknowledges

her colleague's distress with empathy and inquires what upset Alice. It doesn't take long for Alice to feel comforted and tell Sally about her experience. We could also imagine a different narrative for this scenario: Sally does not retain her calm mind–body state but becomes anxious and agitated herself in response to Alice's distress. Most likely, Alice will not calm down and her distress may even increase as a result of their encounter. We rely on co-regulation whenever the intensity of affect and emotional states exceeds or overwhelms our capacity to self-regulate. "Positive" states are no exception—receiving some fantastic news, for example: it is a common impulse to tell a friend and share our excitement.

Most people have others in their lives with whom they feel comfortable to disclose problems or distressing emotions without risking the other person's good esteem. But what about people who are already socially isolated or those who learned to fear negative responses to such disclosures? Or people whose stress phenomena exceed the capacity of families or friends to co-regulate effectively?

Psychotherapy practice has many features in common with traditional healing approaches. All cultures in known history developed niches to facilitate privileged relationships beyond ordinary social or family relations. The archetype of a personal, confiding relationship with a mentor or a helping person is possibly as old as mankind. The birth of psychotherapy owes much to what we would call "medically unexplained symptoms" (MUS) in today's terminology, symptoms for which physicians had found no medical cause. Most of Freud's patients enlisted his help because they were suffering from persistent physical symptoms that defied medical treatments. These symptoms and manifestations included headaches, muscular pain, neuralgia, gastric pain, tics, vomiting, clonic spasms, petit mal, or epileptoid convulsions.

Freud and other physicians of his time came to the conclusion that such symptoms did not have biological or heredity causes but originated in their patients' emotional lives—and specifically in the traumatic events which Freud identified at the root of their complaints. Psychotherapy was effectively born when Freud transformed Breuer's "talking cure" by marrying it with Charcot's notion of traumatic hysteria (Yovall, 2000) and his own techniques for clinical work with repressed memories.

Today, we have a range of clinical constructs to consider and work with the phenomenological spectrum of Charcot's traumatic hysteria, for example borderline personality disorder, or dissociative, somatisation, conversion, and post-traumatic stress disorders. By responding to the Psyche's yet unexplained but demonstrably intolerable distress, Freud, Breuer, Janet, and other pioneers of psychological trauma theory laid the foundations for present-day understanding of severe stress phenomena and their impact on human vitality and functioning.

"Shell-shock", first diagnosed during the First World War, illustrates our Psyche's tribulations when we cannot tolerate the intolerable. Shell-shock phenomena were initially interpreted as disturbances of cerebrospinal fluids caused by close vicinity to bursting shells, or simply dismissed as cowardice, but eventually came to be seen as a psychiatric illness, resulting from injury to the nerves during combat, that required treatment. In a review of original psychoanalytic approaches to traumatic memories, Yovall (2000) highlights how the characteristic features of "shell-shock" such as dissociative spells, memory disturbances, crippling anxiety, vivid nightmares, paralysis, and mutism, match those of Charcot's "traumatic hysteria" in every aspect.

Symptomatologies displayed by shell-shock patients are documented in film footage recorded by two Royal Army neurologists in 1917 (Seale Hayne, 1918). These symptoms must be seen in their contemporary psychosocial context: physicians and military commanders lacked understanding of the causes and effects of traumatic stress, and those affected had few, if any, abilities to articulate their plight. The involuntary movements and autonomic embodiments fly in the face of early twentieth-century military drill and most effectively signal these patients' state of unfitness for soldiering. It is hard to imagine that anybody would consider handing such patients firearms or to give them military tasks. The "war neurosis" footage vividly demonstrates our limitations to suppress or control the Psyche's afflictions, and these soldiers' symptoms may have been their best means to communicate their very acute distress to the military establishment.

A report from a British government inquiry on shell-shock published in 1922 (Imperial War Museum, 2004) concluded that good results could be obtained with the simplest forms of "psycho-therapy" in a majority of cases. Recommendations included two treatment factors that both continue to be seen as key features for contemporary psychotherapy today:

- Each individual case of war neurosis should be treated on its merits.
- The significance of the personality of the physician and their skills in establishing an atmosphere of cure as the basis of all successful treatment.

Today, we have gained more in-depth understanding of human psychobiology and further evidence of how personal experience and meaning become metabolised in physiology and behaviour (Broom, 2007). But the continued prevalence of medically unexplained symptoms in primary care suggests a need for further development in public health services. The stories of human existence are inextricably entwined with physiological phenomena. Abdominal pains, headaches, muscle and joint pains are the most common MUS symptoms, leading to staggering long-term costs for societies and the public purse: in Britain, MUS are estimated to account for thirty per cent of primary care, fifty per cent of secondary care consultations, and eleven per cent of adult healthcare costs. MUS often lead to long-term disabilities.

While severe distress or MUS affect a limited number of people, the impact of emotional illiteracy is evident across society. Emotional literacy is probably the biggest casualty of the common dichotomies mentioned at the start of this chapter. Emotional illiteracy affects a majority of the population: people who struggle to speak about or articulate feelings and emotional experiences. Orbach defines emotional literacy as the capacity to register, recognise, and reflect on emotional states: "Emotional literacy means being able to recognise what you are feeling so that it doesn't interfere with thinking" (1999, p. 84). Orbach highlights the significance of emotions as a facility to draw upon for decision-making or to evaluate situations. Emotional literacy is not identical with emotional expression, which can drive people to act without thinking or get in the way of thinking. People who take time to recognise and reflect on their feelings are usually more in command of themselves than those who cannot.

Neuroscience established that emotions are central for rational functioning and play an indispensable role for our abilities to make sound decisions (Damasio, 1994). Immunology research shows the mental and physical health benefits associated with articulating upsetting experiences and telling our story (Pennebaker, 2003). The benefits of disclosure observed include immune functions, lower levels of depression, lower pain levels and medication use among sufferers of arthritis and asthma, and can be measured regardless of education, ethnicity, culture, or class. But in the public spaces of modern societies or in today's school curricula, emotional literacy remains as ignored and marginal as ever.

Emotional literacy is rarely a reason to seek psychotherapy, but often becomes relevant when the therapeutic focus is less on managing distressing symptoms and more on gaining insights into hidden factors of behaviours or distress that we seek to modify. Dragert (2011) describes how attending to the Psyche may involve a descent into our inner world, a descent that may also lead us towards dark, frightening, or disturbing aspects of our internal world. By facing those dark aspect of life, we may retrieve ignored, rejected, or forgotten parts of ourselves and, much like the story of Psyche in Greek mythology, ultimately emerge more mature and better equipped to live with ourselves and others.

Psychotherapy developed both as an instrument to explore the human experience and as an enabling technique. Depth-psychology provides comprehensive theories about human nature, motivation, behaviour, development, and experience. The change processes commonly seen in psychotherapy are facilitated by patients/clients developing new abilities to recognise and reflect on their experience and by maintaining relationships supportive of this. All forms of psychotherapy utilise interpersonal dynamics and interactions as a vehicle for change. Therapeutic relationships and the therapeutic space they create are crucial tools to help foster the kinds of self-awareness and behaviour change people are seeking to develop. Frank (1971) identified six characteristic features of psychotherapy practice that apply to all psychotherapy modalities:

1. An intense, emotionally charged, confiding relationship with a helping person, or with a group.
2. A rationale, or myth, which includes an explanation of the cause of the patient's distress and a method for relieving it. To be effective, the therapy rationale must be compatible with the cultural worldview shared by patient and therapist to supply a shared scheme for naming and conceptualising symptoms.
3. Re-framing the patient's perceptions of the nature and sources of their problems.

4. Arousal of the patient's hopes for success and strengthening their expectations of help through the personal qualities, status, and work setting of the therapist.
5. Providing success experiences which implicitly or explicitly change the patient's image of themselves, from a person who is overwhelmed by their symptoms and problems, to one who can master them.
6. Facilitating emotional arousal as a prerequisite to attitudinal and behavioural changes.

Depth-psychology also developed therapeutic approaches that specifically utilise social dynamics commonly found in group or family environments. Group therapies, family therapy, or therapeutic communities seek to explore both a person's inner world and any psychosocial dimensions through that person's interactions with others in the room and utilise influences of the whole environment to foster self-awareness and behaviour change.

Psychotherapy cannot cure the Psyche's distress or suffering in the ways we expect a physician to set a broken bone. The goal of psychotherapy is not to eradicate human distress, suffering, or misery in the way we may strive to eradicate malaria. But the psychotherapeutic endeavour offers a viable means to restore hope for a person, to develop new skills and recover our vitality, and bring ourselves back into a more harmonious relationship with ourselves and our environment, with our families and social networks. While psychotherapy cannot "make better" in many instances, it can help with coming to terms with conditions that are difficult to bear. One of Irvin Yalom's best-selling case vignettes ends at his patient's death bed with the poignant exclamation: "Thank you. Thank you for saving my life" (1989, p. 86). Research analysing patient feedback confirmed that all factors identified as "positive outcomes" are profoundly personal and subjective (Fonagy, Jennings-Hobbs, & Sleed, 2012).

## Psyche and Agora

Competing agendas of socialisation versus personal autonomy and self-acceptance create complex tensions between our internal and external priorities. Social, political, and cultural norms promote cooperative social behaviours. These typically require that we sacrifice self-disclosure and self-actualisation or restrict emotional expression for the sake of social inclusion and acceptance.

Societal attitudes towards behaviours perceived as unreasoned, aberrant, or deviant by society are often linked to discomfort, intolerance, or fear. In seventeenth- and eighteenth-century Europe, for example, people suffering emotional upheaval or displaying symptoms attributed to insanity were commonly seen as demon-possessed or characterised as senseless animals and subjected to degrading treatments and deplorable physical or mental abuse. Perceptions and attitudes only improved when social campaigners achieved better recognition of mental illness in the twentieth century. But European societies continued to deprive patients of their dignity and freedom, while psychologists and physicians sought in vain to identify causal factors that determine challenging behaviours and devise treatments capable of modifying them. The catalogue of failed cures ranges from behavioural conditioning programmes to neurological treatments such as the electric shocks immortalised by the film *One Flew Over the Cuckoo's Nest*. Today, stigma and discrimination directed at so-called "mental health problems" such as depression remain widespread in Europe and act as barriers to seeking help or to social participation (Lasalvia et al., 2012).

But societal attitudes towards irregular behaviours can vary greatly between cultures. Historically, Eastern cultures have shown less inclination to discriminate against or incarcerate challenging behaviours. Symptoms of psychic distress or aberrant behaviours are interpreted in a variety of ways, as spiritual afflictions, for example, and largely managed within local communities. Research data highlight the essential role of social integration for our well-being and mental health. Studies commissioned by the World Health Organization over a thirty-year period came to the astonishing conclusion that schizophrenia patients have a significantly better chance to make a full recovery in India, Nigeria, or Columbia compared to Denmark, Britain, or the United States. The comparatively low recovery rate in Western countries despite access to costly biomedical treatment suggests that something essential to recovery is missing in the social fabric of high-income societies (Jablensky & Sartorius, 2008). Social isolation appears to be a key contributing factor to low recovery rates.

But recovery expectations held by patients, carers, and their social environments appear equally key to recovery outcomes. Recovery expectations are informed by cultural belief systems and these vary significantly between societies. The negative prognosis for schizophrenia in Western cultures is based on medical views that mental illnesses constitute degenerative brain disorders and associated perceptions that genuine recovery from schizophrenia is rare. Data from several longitudinal studies indicate that patients who stopped taking their prescribed psychiatric drugs can show vastly improved rates of achieving full recovery compared to patients compliant with psychiatric treatment (Williams, 2012). Williams argues that such recoveries are facilitated by these patients' beliefs in the possibility of real recovery and by developing meanings and more hopeful understandings of their psychotic experiences.

Politicians of all persuasions all too often view unhappiness and personal autonomy as dissension or as threats to the political *status quo*, power, and control. In the early eighteenth century, the philosopher Mandeville challenged classical and Christian ideas that regarded society as a predestined fertile soil wherein the seeds of goodness would grow and flourish. Controversially, Mandeville's *Fable of the Bees* proposed the paradoxical notion that "private vices are public benefits". The fable shows a society that achieves all desired virtues but falls into apathy and becomes utterly paralysed. Mandeville viewed "pride" and "self-love" as instrumental to the way mankind becomes sociable and saw an absence of self-love as the death of progress. Such discourse seems curiously amiss in today's world, where most countries privilege the interests of multinational corporations above the well-being of society.

The tensions and fault-lines between societal and personal realms are complex and multidimensional. In return for cooperative behaviours, societies promise social inclusion—unless you are on society's margins: most societies in history conjured social exclusion for people designated by some lower status such as "untouchables", slaves, or immigrants. Periodically, vulnerable people in society are also targeted as part of some political gambit. In twenty-first-century Britain, social cohesion is coming increasingly under threat through a reckless political agenda to demonise people in need of societal support with a sufficiently brush broad to stoke intolerance for disabilities and mental health problems.

Giving attention to the Psyche is often criticised as inward-looking, or as cultivating vulnerability, or simply dismissed as navel-gazing. But our social networks are rarely robust enough to provide continued and sufficient support when extraordinary events shatter our capacities to cope. There are limitations to the help and support that peers and communities can provide. It doesn't take much—a serious accident, bullying at work, or the death of a close family member, for example—for us to fall through the safety net of our communities and find ourselves isolated. Stolorow (2007) identified isolation as a key feature of trauma, and it is no coincidence that most people who seek psychotherapy share this single common feature.

But is the Psyche really at odds with collective endeavours such as political and cultural activities or social and environmental movements? When classic Greek philosophers distinguished the deeply personal dimension of the individual from its collective tribal environment, they did not propose that the Psyche could flourish in isolation from Agora, the market place. The notion of the personal as some "apolitical" realm is yet another dualistic artefact but may also reflect that many psychotherapists ignore what Samuels (1993) termed the "political Psyche". If we cultivate the Psyche's emotionally reflective capacity, however, we can add emotional depth to political debate and in turn cultivate political reflectiveness in society. In psycho-physiological terms, the two branches of the autonomic nervous system are not in competition with one another but function complementarily—one oriented towards the external, facilitating competition, innovation, and survival; the other towards the internal, facilitating reflection but also collaboration and connection with others.

What is Agora, what is society, but a collaborative joint endeavour of the Psyche? At the turn of the century, neuroscience and social psychology dismantled Descartes' notion of an abstract human nature. "I think, therefore I am" turned into "I feel, therefore I am" (Damasio, 1994) but also into "I am linked, therefore I am" (Gergen, 2002)—statements that attest to a quintessentially personal *and* social-relational nature of human existence.

## New science and the Psyche

There is mounting frustration with a cultural ethos that treats mind, body, and soul as separated compartments or entities. The immunologist and psychotherapist Broom (2007) argues for an unbroken continuity between internal body processes and external interpersonal meanings and influences. Psycho-social meanings play a large role in illness and well-being and in the development of disease, which is usually multifactorial and multidimensional, Broom argues. In Chapter Six, Michael Musalek makes a compelling case to extend the currently dominant evidence-based paradigm towards a human-based paradigm.

The relationship between mind and body, between soma and the Psyche, is pluralistic and mutual rather than top-down and hierarchical. We need a body to think and feel with, Damasio (1994) observed. The systems in the body that form part of the process we call mind include immune, autonomic, and motor systems, and researchers continue to identify previously unrecognised links and mutual inter-dependencies, as Table 1 illustrates.

---

Table 1. Some psychosomatic properties of biological systems.

---

**Kinesthetic activities** are increasingly seen at the core of both subjective experience and abstract thought. They account for a universal use of physical metaphors which connect the mind with the world through the subjectivities of the body (Cozolino, 2006). The unique flow of everyday movement patterns establishes people's disposition to relate to their environments. (Luria, 1973; Sheets-Johnstone, 1999, 2010). Habitual but nonetheless dynamic patterns of movement facilitate a sense of "self-in-action" (Carroll, 2011) and form elastic repertoires of identity and selfhood. Kinesthetic cognition skills support essential life skills such as referencing previous experiences to assess situations and environments, to consider our action potential in any given context, and to choose actions accordingly (Gallese & Sinigaglia, 2011). Adapting more assertive body postures can cause neuroendocrine changes, increase risk tolerance, and lead to behavior change (Carney, Cuddy & Yap, 2010). Other research points to profound influences of kinesthetic activities on learning and memory functions (van Praag, 2009).

**Autonomic nervous system** (ANS) responses serve as regulators of behavior but also determine a person's cognitive responses to any event, ranging from "either-or" cognition driven by sympathetic arousal to "both-and" cognitive responses (Uvnäs-Moberg, 2011) facilitated by the parasympathetic nervous system's quintessentially connective and integrative orientation. ANS responses are interwoven into higher level social, relational, learning and self-regulatory processes (Porges, 2001) but also mutually co-regulated in our relationships with others. (Schore, 1994).

The **immune system** shares a common goal to establish and maintain self-identity with neurological and psychological domains (Booth & Davison, 2003). Immunologists use complex systems modeling approaches to explore the significance of self and non-self discrimination exercised by the immune system which is increasingly seen as an integrative, cognitive system that continually maintains a coherent relationship between self and context (Andrews & Timmis, 2007).

---

The Psyche appears to be "enmattered" in perpetual continuity across physiological, psychological, and social layers of existence. Disturbances on any level, psychic, corporeal, or social, will inevitably impact all other dimensions too. Psychosomatic and biopsychosocial medicine assert that Psyche and soma cannot really be isolated for practical or theoretical purposes, and instead offer systemic models whereby multiple biological, psychological, and social factors are seen as interlinked. Metzinger (2003) considers self-hood functions as instruments for homeostatic self-regulation. A divided or dissociative self is deeply impairing for our abilities to function.

A mounting body of evidence suggests that higher-order forms of subjectivity enable us to speculate, make judgements based on qualitative factors, and modify our possible actions accordingly. In recent decades, we have seen a growing ascendancy of neuroscientific research and interpretations of human behaviour. But neuroscience is unlikely to provide all the answers required, and we may be a long way from even understanding what a science of consciousness might be a science of. Classic science has proven ill-equipped to effectively investigate higher-order forms of subjectivity. Current paradigm shifts listed by Carroll in Table 2 are steadily transforming classical science towards a new science framework that appears better suited to investigate phenomenological subjectivities.

Biological systems such as hormonal, immune, autonomic, and motor systems operate memory acquisition and learning processes. System theories such as chaos, complexity, and field theory are better suited to deal with complexities (Carroll, 2011). They can describe complex events were a great many variables are interacting with each other, while avoiding the traps of dualistic thinking associated with conceptual frameworks that focus on structures and functions.

Scientists investigating the neuroscience of consciousness and free will are grappling with data showing that neurological signals are preceded by the motor activities they are thought to initiate. Seen through a classic science lens, such data could suggest that consciousness may be only epiphenomenal and illusory. From a system theory perspective, however, such data may confirm a mutually interactive bottom-up and top-down flow or, in Sheets-Johnstone's words, describe how "movement forms the I that moves before the I that moves forms movement" (1999, pp. 137–138). Researchers expect that quantum biology will eventually explain such data (Hameroff, 2012).

Table 2. Classical versus new science.

| Classical science | New science |
| --- | --- |
| Causality | Emergent properties |
| Linear | Non-linear |
| Objective | Includes subjectivity |
| Isolates events | Emphasizes context |
| Matter | Process |
| Focuses on stability | Focuses on sensitivity |
| Logic | Deeper pattern |
| Closed system | Open system |
| Reductive | Complex |
| Predictability | Chaos |
| Explicit/observable | Implicit/hidden |
| Time is uniform | Sensitive critical periods |
| Cause-effect | Feedback loops |
| Sequential | Experience-dependent |
| Mechanistic | Self-regulating |
| Fixed relations | Self-organizing |
| Objects (physical) | Fields |
| Particulate | Parallel |

Carroll (2003, p. 194). Reproduced with permission of the copyright owner.

When a self-experiencing system acquires a certain complexity, Metzinger (2003) argues, it becomes a necessity for the system as a whole to explain its own inner and outer actions to itself. It needs to monitor and "own" itself and its own history and predict its own future behaviours with the aid of internal simulation facilities. This would necessarily require some computational tools that helps the system to own its own hardware. But should we assume that such tools would constitute or represent the system that owns the tool?

## Conclusions

Whether we define the Psyche as a soul, as self-hood, identity, or a phenomenal self, it is almost certainly not simply some brain-based phenomena. On the contrary, the Psyche may turn out to constitute a shared property and function of our entire organism. Instead of "not associated with *any* organ of the organism", as the classic Greek conception proposed, the Psyche may be intimately associated with *all* organs and cell structures. As a shared property and function of the entire human organism, the Psyche must necessarily also include social correlates—the narrative of identity is social-relational as well as corporeal. Psyche, soma, and Agora, our social world, are inextricably bound to one another.

The classic notion of the Psyche and its depth-psychology expansion has yet to be refuted. On the other hand, our conception of the Psyche may become further refined and expanded with the aid of already existing, or yet to be formulated, new-science paradigms. The Psyche's phenomenology and phenomenological subjectivities have eluded the classic sciences in their search for measurable data and objectivities. But can society afford to maintain the myth that biochemical circuits or strings of DNA alone will eventually deliver some magic key to unlock human nature and behaviour, and continue to ignore the very subjectivities that make us human and form the basis of social phenomena?

## References

Abad, G. (2003). Early Greek lyric poetry: the cry of the self. Singapore Management University http://ink.library.smu.edu.sg/soss_research/15/ (accessed on 28 August 2014).

Alexander, C. (1979). *The Timeless Way of Building*. New York: Oxford University Press.

Angell, M. (2011). The epidemic of mental illness: why? *The New York Review of Books*, 23 June.

Bennett, A. (2004). *The History Boys*. London: Faber.

Booth, R. J., & Davison, K. P. (2003). Relating to our worlds in a psychobiological context: the impact of disclosure on self generation and immunity. In: J. N. Wilce (Ed.), *Social and Cultural Lives of Immune Systems*. London: Routledge.

Broom, B. C. (2007). *Meaning-Full Disease: How Personal Experience and Meanings Initiate and Maintain Physical Illness*. London: Karnac.

Brown, B. C. (2010). *The Gifts of Imperfection: Let Go of Who You Think You're Supposed To Be and Embrace Who You Are*. Center City, MN: Hazelden.

Carney, D., Cuddy, A., & Yap, A. (2010). Power posing: brief nonverbal displays affect neuroendocrine levels and risk tolerance. *Psychological Science, 21(10)*: 1363–1368.

Carroll, R. (2003). On the border between chaos and order. In: J. Corrigall & H. Wilkinson (Eds.), *Revolutionary Connections: Psychotherapy and Neuroscience*. London: Karnac.

Carroll, R. (2011). In search of a vocabulary of embodiment. *Body, Movement and Dance in Psychotherapy, 6*: 245–257.

Cooper, M. (2013). Keynote at the International Humanistic Psychology Conference. London, 7 September.

Cozolino, L. (2006). *The Neuroscience of Human Relationships: Attachment and the Developing Brain*. London: Norton.

Damasio, A. R. (1994). *Descartes' Error*. New York: Grosset/Putnam.

Damasio, A. R. (2010). *Self Comes to Mind*. London: Vintage.

Dragert, G. (2011). Defining psychotherapy. *The Psychotherapist, 48*: 27–29.

Fonagy, P., Jennings-Hobbs, R., & Sleed, M. (2012). Coming home to ourselves: evaluating the outcomes of counselling provided by ICAP. http://www.icap.org.uk (accessed 3 September 2012).

Frank, J. D. (1971). Therapeutic factors in psychotherapy. *American Journal of Psychotherapy, 25*: 350–361.

Gallese, V., & Sinigaglia, C. (2011). How the body in action shapes the self. *Journal of Consciousness Studies, 18(7–8)*: 117–143.

Hameroff, S. (2012). How quantum brain biology can rescue conscious free will. *Frontiers Integrative Neuroscience, 6*: 93.

Hillman, J. (1964). *Suicide and the Soul*. London: Hodder & Stoughton.

Hillman, J. (1976). *Revisioning Psychology*. New York: Harper-Perennial.

Imperial War Museum (2004). *The Report of the War Office Committee of Enquiry into Shell-Shock*. London: Imperial War Museum.

Jablensky, A., & Sartorius, N. (2008). What did the WHO studies really find? *Schizophrenia Bulletin, 34(2)*: 253–255.

Keleman, S. (1985). *Emotional Anatomy*. Berkeley, CA: Center Press.

Lasalvia, A., Zoppei, S., Van Bortel, T., Bonetto, C., Cristofalo, D., Wahlbeck, K., Bacle, S. V., Van Audenhove, C., van Weeghel, J., Reneses, B., Germanavicius, A., Economou, M., Lanfredi, M., Ando, S., Sartorius, N., Lopez-Ibor, J. J., Thornicroft, G.; ASPEN/INDIGO Study Group (2012). Global pattern of experienced and anticipated discrimination reported by people with major depressive disorder: a cross-sectional survey. *The Lancet, 18.10.12*.

Luria, A. R. (1973). *The Working Brain*. London: Penguin.

Metzinger, T. (2003). *Being No One: The Self-Model Theory of Subjectivity*. London: MIT.

Orbach, S. (1999). *Towards Emotional Literacy*. London: Virago.

Pennebaker, J. W. (2003). Telling stories: the health benefits of disclosure. In: J. N. Wilce (Ed.), *Social and Cultural Lives of Immune Systems*. London: Routledge.

Porges, S. W. (2001). The polyvagal theory: phylogenetic substrates of a social nervous system. *International Journal of Psychophysiology, 42*: 123–146.

Rhode, E. (1925). *Psyche: The Cult of Souls and the Belief in Immortality among the Greeks* (Trans. W. B. Hillis). London: Routledge & Kegan Paul (Reprinted from Psyche: Seelencult und Unsterblichkeitsglaube der Griechen. Leibzig 1894).

Samuels, A. (1993). *The Political Psyche*. London: Routledge.

Schore, A. (1994). *Affect Regulation and the Origin of the Self: The Neurobiology of Emotional Development*. Hillsdale, NJ: Lawrence Erlbaum.

Seale Hayne Military Hospital (1918). *War Neuroses* [electronic resource]: *Netley Hospital, 1917*. London: Wellcome Trust, 2008.

Sheets-Johnstone, M. (1999). *The Primacy of Movement*. Amsterdam/ Philadelphia: John Benjamins.

Sheets-Johnstone, M. (2010). *Putting Movement into Your Life: A Beyond Fitness Primer*. Amazon Kindle Edition.

Society for Humanistic Psychology (2012). *Open Letter to the DSM-5*. http:// dsm5-reform.com/ (accessed on 21 March 2013).

Stolorow, R. D. (2007). *Trauma and Human Existence: Autobiographical, Psychoanalytic and Philosophical Reflections*. New York: Analytic Press.

Uvnäs-Moberg, K. (2011). *The Oxytocin Factor: Tapping the Hormone of Calm, Love and Healing* (2nd edn.). London: Pinter & Martin.

van Praag, H. (2009). Exercise and the brain: something to chew on. *Trends in Neurosciences, 32(5)*: 283–290.

Williams, P. (2012). *Rethinking Madness: Towards a Paradigm Shift in Our Understanding and Treatment of Psychosis*. San Rafael, CA: Sky's Edge Publishing.

Yalom, I. D. (1989). *Love's Executioner and Other Tales of Psychotherapy*. London: Penguin.

# CHAPTER TWO

# The politics of intelligence: working with intellectual disability

*Alan Corbett*

## Introduction

Intelligence has become the cornerstone of how we judge ourselves and others, and society's relationship with intelligence elevates cognitive ability at the expense of other phenomena, such as affect and emotion. In Western societies, intelligence is a lens through which we see and interact with our world, and its measurement has become a political as much as a social practice. In this chapter, I will explore the notion of intelligence—how we conceptualise and measure it, and how these measurements affect where those with low intelligence are located within society. Through an examination of the way in which the psychotherapeutic profession has tended to avoid engaging with patients with disabilities, I will consider what it is about intelligence that can evoke in others feelings of fear, disdain, and confusion, and how we seem to need to idealise intelligence while denigrating disability. Taking consent as a metaphor for how we relate to and understand those with intellectual disabilities, I will consider the notion of working with intellectual disability as being, at its heart, a fundamentally political act, the avoidance of which results in our own fears concerning mental frailty, cognitive deterioration, and difference being projected aggressively and unfairly into those with disabilities.

## Measures of intelligence?

Definitions of intelligence as the ability to adapt to change, or that intelligence serves the main purpose of adaptation to the environment, found widespread agreement over the course of the twentieth century (Sternberg & Detterman, 1986). Jensen (1998) identifies a general factor of intelligence, often referred to as the *g* factor, that underlies all adaptive behaviour. Gardner's theory of multiple intelligences (1983) suggests eight separate intelligences: linguistic, logical-mathematical, spatial, musical, bodily kinaesthetic, interpersonal, intrapersonal, and naturalistic.

Kaufman and Singer (2004) built upon this concept, formulating additional intelligence categories, such as spiritual and existential. They also describe these domains of cognitive functioning in terms of "successful intelligence", with Sternberg adding that "success is attained through a balance of analytical, creative, and practical abilities" (1997, pp. 297–298). "Analytical intelligence" refers to the capacities to analyse and examine problems. This appears insufficient in isolation. In the absence of "creative intelligence", the ability to create solutions remains out of reach. People with autism, for example, may know much about the dimensions of a problem, but only in a terribly concretised, uncreative way. Strauman and Higgins (1987) point to the importance of creative intelligence in the light of discrepancies between a patient's view of their actual core self and their ideal, imagined self. It is the failure of creative intelligence to provide some pathway between the actual and the imagined self that can, in their view, lead to depression. "Practical intelligence" is needed to augment our creative abilities if we want to utilise our ideas and our analysis effectively.

Gardner (1983) differentiated "intrapersonal intelligence", the ability to access one's own emotional life from "interpersonal intelligence", the ability to read the moods, intentions, and desires of others. His formulation regards the personal intelligences as biologically based information-processing capacities—one directed inward, the other directed outward—but intimately entwined. This connects with Salovey and Mayer's (1990) concept of emotional intelligence, latterly defined as "the ability to perceive and express emotion, assimilate emotion in thought, understand and reason with emotion, and regulate emotion in the self and others" (Mayer et al., 2000, p. 396). Mead described the "whole nature of intelligence as social to its very core" (1934, p. 141) and like Synder (1994) considered the primary aspect of human intelligence to be the capacity of the individual to "put himself in the place of another".

## Measuring intelligence

The most common method for measuring intelligence is the Intelligence Quotient (IQ) test by which patients are herded into one of several categories, those falling under the mark of seventy being diagnosed as having an intellectual disability. Whitaker (2006) found that fourteen per cent of IQs changed by ten points or more from one assessment to the next and points to Flynn finding the average IQ of the population as a whole going up by about three points a decade. Therefore, tests that were standardised several years ago would give higher IQ than tests standardised today. As time goes on since the test was standardised, the proportion of the population assessed as having an IQ of less than seventy will have gradually decreased. People may be wrongly diagnosed as having an intellectual disability or not being diagnosed when they should have been. Intellectual disability diagnosis also relies on measurements of adaptive behaviour and social functioning that are subject to concerning margins of error (Whitaker, 2008).

IQ testing promises to produce an "objective" and "infallible" measure of intelligence. Its current indomitable status in the psychological world was born in the context of migration, the growth of mass education, and the need to rank populations by intelligence. Historically, IQ tests have been used as a tool to segregate the intelligent from the intellectually disabled and to decide whether people were allowed to immigrate, to reproduce, and, in the most extreme cases of politically informed eugenics, whether people lived or died (Murdoch, 2009).

## Intellectual disability and society

The pre-Enlightenment age viewed people with intellectual disability (and with mental illnesses) as having a value in society (Gilbert, 2006). Monasteries throughout Europe provided asylum and care for people with intellectual disabilities in a manner we could describe as the first welfare system in Europe. Despite its tendency to view those with disabilities in an infantilised way, as "objects of pity" (Wolfensberger, 1992), this system provided a level of care and support for those at the margins of medieval life in ways that should shame the architects of the current, ideologically driven, slashing of disability services in Britain today. It was only with the dawn of the "Age of Reason" and the Industrial Revolution in the eighteenth and nineteenth centuries, that people began to be judged more for their potential economic contribution towards society. People with disabilities, with their perceived inability to produce and contribute, began to be viewed as a burden in increasingly individualistic and utilitarian societies (Gilbert, 2006).

## Psychotherapy and intelligence

The psychotherapy field incorporated a number of cultural prejudices, as some of the other chapters highlight, and societal disdain for those with intellectual disabilities is no exception. Few twentieth-century clinicians expressed interest in providing psychotherapy for people with intellectual disabilities, perhaps following Freud's dictum about "a certain measure of natural intelligence" being a prerequisite for treatment (Freud, 1904). One analyst to challenge this prevailing view was Pierce Clark (1933), who is best known for his work on epilepsy, but who made a major contribution to an analytic understanding of intellectual disability. O'Driscoll (2009) suggests that Clark's early death prevented a dissemination of psychotherapeutic theorising in the treatment of such patients and led to a dearth of clinical writing on intellectual disability throughout most of the twentieth century.

The late twentieth century saw a number of clinicians examining intellectual disability from a psychoanalytic perspective, most notably Sinason (1992). In a pivotal paper on countertransference with mentally handicapped clients, Symington (1992) highlights the phenomena of disdain and contempt towards disabled patients, as evidenced in the reactions of participants at a "mental handicap" workshop, where clinicians shared their observations of differences that distinguished their work with intellectually disabled patients from that with other patients. With disabled patients, they were far more likely to continue a discussion with a colleague in the corridor while a patient was waiting for the session to begin. Participants became aware of their tendencies to dress down on days when they were working with patients with disabilities, caring less about how they appeared to their patients. Symington links these responses to eugenics, the murderous intent of the Nazi party, and to the animal kingdom, where a flock of birds may attack and kill the one that is wounded.

Disability therapy is an endeavour saturated by a complex amalgam of fear, confusion, and hatred. Our unconscious fear of and hatred for disability is enacted in a dissociative professional response by which our consulting room doors, as much as the doors of our training institutions, are shut and bolted against those whose brains work too differently from our own. With notable exceptions, practitioners and theoreticians have chosen to treat only those whose intelligence fits certain selective criteria. As a profession, we have been forced to view historical antipathies to working with other ethnic and sexual minorities as evidence of unacceptable prejudice. Locking the consulting room door against those with disabilities continues to be seen as acceptable and remains a largely unchallenged form of discrimination.

Such intelligence prejudice affects not only the intellectually disabled, however. Schofield observed that many of the therapists he supervised showed a tendency to favour working with certain patients over others. In *Psychotherapy: The Purchase of Friendship*, he wrote:

> What is there in the general theory of psychodynamics or psychotherapy to suggest that the neurosis of a 50-year-old commercial fisherman with an eighth-grade education will be more resistant to psychological help than a symptomatically comparable disturbance in a 35-year-old, college-trained artist? … It seems … likely that there are pressures toward a systematic selection of patients, pressures that are perhaps subtle and unconscious in part and that, in part, reflect theoretical biases common to all psychotherapists. These selective forces tend to restrict the efforts of the bulk of social workers, psychologists, and psychiatrists to clients who present the "Yavis" syndrome—clients who are **youthful, attractive, verbal, intelligent and successful**. (1964, p. 133; bold added by editor)

Hopper (2012, p. 230) raises another common issue about disability therapy when he writes:

> Our colleagues do not always get much gratification from their limited clinical achievement Although it is marvellous when a learning disabled patient has a breakthrough in, for example, his capacity to reflect upon his actions and gain some sense of having a mind of his own, this is often a consolation prize. In contrast to some clinical presentations which may begin with a mention of a client's high intelligence, we cannot present our cases by saying "Of course, he is highly stupid, in fact as thick as two planks". In

other words, we cannot identify with the brilliant but must find other sources of gratification in our work. (Actually, is there a point of saying that a patient is highly intelligent? To illustrate that the patient is unable to realize his potential? Or to convey that the patient is unable to use our brilliant interpretation?)

There is a reluctance at the heart of psychoanalysis to examine the aetiology of its aversion to working with those whose brains represent something other. Collectively, we have adopted defence mechanisms common in Western societies with which to rationalise our unthinking terror of, and disdain for, the intellectually disabled. Our formulations of treatability in relation to patients with intellectual disabilities have privileged the cognitive above the relational, causing a non-thinking paralysis within the psychoanalytic profession. In order to examine ways of unravelling this paralysis, I want to illustrate some common dilemmas with the aid of an anonymised clinical vignette. Through this, I wish to examine the notion of consent as being a metaphor for our societal attitudes towards people with intellectual disabilities.

## Vignette

It is a grey Monday morning in Dublin. I am waiting to meet a man about whom I know little. The facts I have are that he:

- is in his fifties,
- has an intellectual disability,
- lives in a home run by a religious order,
- has a sexual history that, for some reason, has caused others to consider him a risk to others.

It is an odd set of facts to know about someone, particularly the fact of his sexual history, and I find myself reflecting on the things I do not know—such as what he looks like, what kind of family he comes from, and what he thinks about coming to see me. The final omission is a key one and were I will focus this morning. Today is the first part of an assessment process to ascertain whether this man, whom I will call "Seamus", wants to attend a therapy group I am co-conducting, and whether he is suitable for the group. This is a psychotherapy group for people with intellectual disabilities who have "problems with relationships", which tends to be a euphemism to describe people who have exhibited worrying sexual behaviour.

THE POLITICS OF INTELLIGENCE

I want to work out how much Seamus knows about why he is coming to see me today, and how much he is consenting to this session. I know that Seamus may well enter the room knowing nothing about me or the group. This is one of the factors that differentiates disability psychotherapy from psychotherapy with the non-disabled (Hinshelwood, 1991). Most patients research the kind of therapist they wish to see, what training they have had, or the fees they charge. None of these questions have, presumably, been asked by Seamus.

I hear him enter the centre. He is accompanied by someone I will call "Mary", a member of staff from the home where he lives. I go out to the waiting room and am struck by how anxious both Seamus and Mary look. I introduce myself, and ask Seamus if he is ready to come into the room with me. He looks more nervous, and asks if Mary can come in too, something I agree to.

Once inside the room, I introduce myself again, explaining that I understood Seamus might be interested in coming to a group that is starting here in the coming year. Before the words were out of my mouth, Seamus said, "Yes, yes, I do. I do." The words were spoken with real anxiety, giving me a sense of the way in which Seamus encounters the world, as a dangerous, fearful place that has to be placated and agreed with.

I am aware here of needing to slow him down, to try to stem the tide of anxiety that threatened to overwhelm both him and me. I said a few things about the need to take things slowly and thoughtfully. At this point, Mary asked if she could stay for the entire session, something I said could not happen unless Seamus wanted it to. Seamus said that he would be "grand", at which point Mary said that he was extremely nervous, although at this point she appeared the more anxious of the two.

I then went on to outline the boundaries of the session—how long it would last and how Seamus would be entitled to stop the session at any point if he wished to. Seamus's interjections at this point were tremendously placatory. He repeated that all was "grand" and everything was "right".

I then asked him why he thought he had come today. He said that he was coming "For my nightmares. Nightmares I've been having." I spent some time exploring this, interested as I was in the fact that it appeared to be Seamus's main motivation in being here, wondering about the nightmares' possible connections with sexuality or abuse. Before going deeper into this, I re-iterated some of the ground rules of our session, seeking to ensure that Seamus was briefed properly on what he was entering into. These ground rules mostly concerned confidentiality and safety, and it was striking that his responses to all I was saying continued to be deeply affirmative, assuring me repeatedly that it would be "grand, grand".

I became aware at this point in the session of a rather punitive countertransferential feeling, as if I were somehow torturing Seamus by spending so much time on the rules of the session. I attempted to counter this by slowing down myself, and seeking to allow Seamus more space to explore his feelings. It was around the point that I suggested that Mary could leave the session, if Seamus felt safe enough to stay in the room without her. He said that he did, and after she left, we began to explore Seamus's understanding of my role. I asked him what he might want to know about me, to which he replied (smiling for the first time) "Everything!" It was interesting that Seamus immediately picked up on my reticence about telling him everything (or much at all) about me—born from my desire to protect the boundaries of our work, but serving to illustrate the asymmetric nature of our relationship. I repeated back the word "Everything" to him, but could tell from his response ("Or just bits and pieces") that he remained in compliant, pacifying mode, and wanted to reassure me that he would not be demanding I tell him all about myself.

We went on to explore the nature of the referral to the group, with Seamus being surprisingly clear about which professional had referred him ("Eamonn (a psychologist) … . he's got a beard."). This led us to return to the theme of Seamus's nightmares, and the help he wished to get with them. Through gentle questioning, I got more information from Seamus about his background, and the main emotional milestones of his life. These included the death of his parents, and that of his brother. It was difficult at times to gauge how much to facilitate this alongside the need to clarify the remit of the group, a constant issue in psychotherapy assessments generally and, from my experience, in assessments with people with intellectual disability in particular.

I went on to raise the issue of consent to share information about this session with my co-therapist. I spent some time talking through the reasons for asking, and what it might mean to him. I finished off by stating that I would only be able to have such a conversation with her if he agreed to it. Instantly, Seamus stated, "Yes, you can." I replied,

"I noticed that you said 'yes you can' straight away, and it was like you didn't need to think about it. But here it's really important that you take time to really think about things. You're allowed to say 'no' to things here. You're allowed to say you're not sure. I'm not allowed to do anything without you agreeing to it."

Seamus reassured me again at this point that this was "grand" by him. I found myself wishing to clarify the issue of consent still further, and re-iterated that he was fully entitled to call a halt to the referral, or to my discussing his case with others, or, indeed, to my writing up my clinical notes from the sessions. Each time I paused, Seamus inserted a "That's grand" or "Yes, you can."

My punitive countertransference returned, with a strong sense of bombarding Seamus with an overload of information that simply felt anti-therapeutic. I decided again to rein in my explanation of the boundaries of the sessions in favour of a less structured exploration of Seamus's life.

Using a large piece of paper and markers, we drew various attachment figures in his life, with Seamus conveying a great deal of useful information about the structure of his week. He also told me that he had been seeing a psychiatrist, and had been prescribed some medication. His understanding of this medication was that it was intended to help him with his nightmares. This led us to explore further the kind of help the group might be able to offer him. In closing the session, I checked whether Seamus wished to return the following week to continue our discussion. In doing this, I asked whether he would wish to give his consent to me talking more to Mary about the group, and his place in it. This was a particularly important point, as alongside the therapy group will be a parallel group for workers and family members. It was likely that Mary might be a member of this group. Again, Seamus agreed without hesitation to this. Mary returned to the room. While Seamus left the room to visit the toilet, Mary opened her handbag and brought out a rather tatty-looking piece of paper. "Right", she began, "This is the list of Seamus's medication. He was on one lot for years and he shouldn't have been. That's the Androcur. It was this psychiatrist—there was this incident, you see, and ever since then he's been on it and it had all sorts of side effects and …".

I stopped Mary before she could say any more, explaining that we would need to check with Seamus as to whether he was happy to consent to her giving me this personal information about him. Mary looked furious, and hurt, but was unable to say much more, as Seamus was re-entering the room. We said our farewells, with Seamus grabbing my hand as he left, saying, "I'm glad you're my friend."

The encounter with Seamus and Mary left me with numerous questions that encompass the social, psychotherapeutic, and ethical. My main task was to establish whether Seamus could and would consent to being assessed for a place in a therapy group. At first glance, it would appear that he was consenting. All his responses to my questions about consent were affirmative: "Yes, that's right …. grand, that's grand …. yes, I do …". With people with intellectual disability, however, one cannot presume that such affirmative responses mean the person is actually giving informed consent, for to give informed consent one needs to understand what is being asked. Seamus may have been saying "yes" to everything because he wanted me to like him, or he was scared that something bad might happen to him if he said "no". He may have constructed a view of the world as a place that has to be placated, and all those in it as people to be appeased.

I am aware that I could simply abandon my curiosity in whether Seamus has the capacity to make an informed decision about coming into therapy or not. I could, theoretically, take his "grand, grand" at face value and agree with him that it would be grand for him to come into therapy. After all, I believe that the group will be a good therapeutic space for him. This does not sit well, however, and I become aware of my wish to not align myself with Mary and her propensity to ignore Seamus's autonomy.

In the weeks to come, Seamus returns for sessions, but the nagging suspicion remains that he may more motivated to appease his carers than by any psychotherapy benefits. In one session, I find myself feeling rather infuriated by Seamus's propensity to answer "yes" to everything I suggest. I say, "You do know, don't you Seamus, that instead of saying 'yes' to me, you could sometimes say 'no', or 'I don't know', and I wouldn't be at all upset." Seamus looks at me for a while, thoughtfully, and eventually replies, "OK. No." He stares at me for a while, gauging whether this answer is, in fact, the one I had been wanting to hear.

## Thinking and power

Key to an understanding of intelligence is the issue of power. The instance of Mary suddenly providing lots of unasked-for information about Seamus's medication could indicate an attempt to reclaim some power in what may have been a disempowering professional situation for her. I then attempted to wrest it back from her by insisting on rigid adherence to psychotherapeutic boundaries. What, then, of Seamus's power? How possible will it be for this assessment process to be one that actively empowers him, a process that places him at the centre of things rather than at the margins? Can he seize power in any other way than by absenting himself from the process? Such absence could be achieved by complying superficially but holding back on key aspects of his personal world.

The assessment of people with intellectual disabilities is a tripartite process, involving not only patient and therapist but also the patient's support network. Patients with intellectual disabilities tend not to refer themselves for therapy, being referred either by a social-care professional or a member of their family. They also tend not to pay for their therapy—payment being handled by a third party. Someone else may have the responsibility of getting them to and from the consulting room. So the therapeutic process is a triangulated one, by which the therapist has to locate themselves in proximity to the carer(s) in ways that avoid interfering with the therapeutic relationship.

Assessments need to take into account both internal and external worlds of the patient. For many carers of people with intellectual disabilities, be they paid carers or family members, the opportunity to talk about how they feel about the patient is a rare one. The fact of the question being asked in the service of a psychoanalytic investigation can help a carer examine hitherto unexpressed emotions, such as resentment for the patient, or for their disability, and envy of the care and attention they receive, in stark contrast to the invisibility of many carers' needs.

## Notions of consent

Issues of consent are relevant beyond intellectual disability and the helping professions as modern developments present us with ever-increasing complexities. Notions of informed and uninformed consent can be traced back to the texts of ancient Greece and Byzantium (Dalla-Vorgia et al., 2001), with Plato's exhortation to doctors to explain to patients the extent of their medical condition and the consequences of a course of treatment prior to obtaining their consent. This is consistent with the Platonic epistemology that knowledge is innate—according to Plato the patient knows what is good for him, and thus the physician's role is to help this hidden knowledge emerge through the use of argument

(Lane, 2007). O'Neill (1998) argues against the notion of Hippocrates as an exponent of informed consent and quotes Hippocrates' instructions to *conceal* information from patients. A Hippocratic understanding of consent stems from a belief that the physician is attending not only to the physical but the emotional health of his patient, and should use his power to limit the flow of information that could have a detrimental effect on both.

Power and authority are central to the notion of "therapeutic privilege", a concept O'Neill (1998) ascribes to Percival's influential *Medical Ethics*. Therapeutic privilege was commonly used to justify withholding information from a patient in light of the serious psychological threat such information may present. Katz (2002) positions the power dynamic in the relationship between physician and patient as being integral to an understanding of consent, with a politicised recognition of the passive and dis-empowered position that patients had traditionally been put into through the asymmetric nature of the doctor's role.

Miller, Vandome, and McBrewster (2009) trace the origins of "informed consent" to a 1957 medical malpractice case, although O'Neill (1998) questions the immediate power of the term, suggesting in his analysis the more relevant evolution of terminology from "negative duty" (in which false information to patients is prohibited) to "affirmative duty" (the requirement, formulated in the 1960s, to inform patients of the possible hazards of treatment). He also charts the shift from the "reasonable doctor" standard in 1960 (duty to disclose being limited by the physician being guided by the patient's best therapeutic interests) to the "reasonable patient" standard in 1972 (informed consent founded on the idea of the patient as decision-maker). This is, of course, a highly significant change and one that has been slower to embed itself in clinical practice relating to people with intellectual disabilities—due, I suggest, to the reluctance of many professionals to devolve any of the power invested in them.

### The legacy of Platonic and Hippocratic perspectives

Most debates about consent can be seen to fall somewhere between a Platonic or a Hippocratic position, a helpful framework when examining the contemporary political dimensions of the consent debate within psychotherapy and other helping professions. Despite their analyses being confined within an American bioethical framework, thus robbing their work of some of its transferability to non-Western and, indeed, European societies, Berg and Appelbaum (2001) form useful connections between the patients' rights movement in the late 1960s and 1970s and the women's and civil rights movements, and link the right to determine what happened to one's own body with the concurrent surge against medical paternalism within the prevailing social consensus in the Western world. They introduce a philosophical perspective—that of Kant, who stated that ethics must be governed by respect for others as self-legislating (autonomous) beings. This is contrasted with the prominent ethical theory of utilitarianism, wherein the ethically best option is the one that produces the most overall utility.

Schneider (1998) questions the role of autonomy in informed consent in ways that highlight how equivocal the desire for autonomy sometimes is, an arguably inevitable consequence of desire for control being partial, ambivalent, and complex. Although not explicitly posited, this appears to be also an argument for a more individualistic concept of consent, as much as an argument against the notion that because most people are thought to want to exercise or withdraw informed consent on medical decisions, *all* people do. Schneider's argument against the "mandatory autonomy" view is echoed by Berg and Appelbaum (2001, p. 32), who suggest it is possible to be an "autonomous moral agent without choosing autonomously all the time in every instance".

## Contemporary debates

The past decade has seen an increase in debate about consent in relation to such issues as releasing medical information about the genetic structure of one patient so their family may be armed with information about potentially debilitating conditions in their own genetics (Kent, 2003), working with patients with degenerative conditions such as Alzheimer's (Kim et al., 2001), acquired head injury (Dickinson et al., 2000), patients with HIV (Roberts et al., 2003), and the concept of *presumed consent* (Abadiea & Gayb, 2006; Gill, 2004).

By viewing consent from a disability perspective, we may be able to see with greater clarity the particular impact made on consent negotiations by notions of power and authority. Capacity has been shown to be a functional concept, determined by someone's ability to understand, retain, and weigh up information in order to arrive at and to communicate a choice (Wong et al., 1999). This represents a shift from the previous approach to capacity being based on diagnosis (a person lacking capacity because of membership of a particular diagnostic group) or outcome (a person lacking capacity because he or she makes an unwise decision) (Murphy & O'Callaghan, 2004; Murphy & Clare, 2003).

Bybee and Zigler's (1999) concept of "outerdirectedness", the propensity for people with intellectual disabilities to follow the lead of people without intellectual disabilities has a bearing upon how consent is conceptualised. An asymmetry of power is not exclusive to these patients as it applies in various degrees to all therapeutic relationships (Boyd, 1996). But the issue takes particularly significance in disability therapy where consent may become the most potent container for issues of power and powerlessness in the therapeutic process, and, given how vulnerable our patients are to over-compliance and outer-directedness, emerging as a metaphor for the patient's relationship with their world.

There can be no easy choice between informed or uninformed consent. This is a point I am making not just in relation to patients with intellectual disabilities, but one that can help inform general psychotherapeutic practice as well as other contexts. I have formulated a more nuanced concept of consent (Corbett, 2012) that identifies variants of informed and uninformed consent (Figure 1):

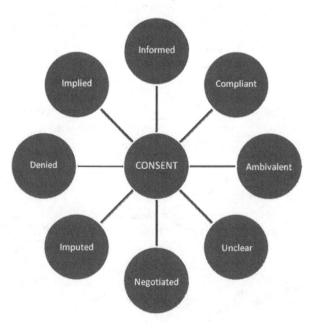

Figure 1. Forms of consent.

Consent is an intersubjective process dependent on a range of conscious and unconscious factors, and coloured by the forces of power and authority implicit within any relational dyad. A propensity for "outer-directedness" impacts upon the agency felt by someone with an intellectual disability, and upon their capacity to demonstrate truly informed consent. The dyad is still "asymmetrical", through one being incumbent on the other (Jayyusi, 1984) due to an imbalance of cognition, power, knowledge, and agency.

Consent can thus be viewed as a metaphor for the way in which we think (and feel) about people with intellectual disabilities. Our societal privileging of intelligence has positioned people with intellectual disabilities at the bottom rung of society's ladder. This is, I suggest, as unhelpful to us as it is unfair to people with intellectual disabilities. It concretises a binary "us or them" view of intelligence, by which our fear of our own intelligence being insufficient, faulty, or vulnerable can be avoided by projecting our terror of our own potential or actual unintelligence into people with intellectual disabilities. They have then a powerful function within society—they become the container for our unthinkable anxieties.

## Conclusions

To have intelligence is to have power. To work with patients with intellectual disabilities forces us to think about our own relationship with intelligence, as much as with power. Psychotherapy privileges intelligence over many other qualities, which, in part, explains the fact that people with intellectual disabilities are missing from the history of this profession. Working with disability means working with one's own disabilities. This is never more alive than in those moments when we are at the receiving end of powerfully disabling projections in sessions, in which our capacity to think, to speak, and to feel is intensely attacked, leading to a powerfully felt "disability transference" (Corbett, 2009). I suggest that this is enacted in psychotherapy on two levels: intrapsychically, within the intimacy of the consulting room, and also systemically, through the historical inability of the psychoanalytic profession to adapt its practice to accommodate the needs of a section of society that tends to be experienced as messy, confusing, and frightening.

This is not exclusively a problem for psychotherapists—it extends to a far wider range of professions. We seem to struggle with unconscious fears that low intelligence is somehow contagious, and that by treating patients with intellectual disabilities, we are risking something we tend to value far higher than other human qualities—our intelligence. We cannot escape the challenges arising from societal dynamics that surround disability in the Western societies. To work with people with intellectual disabilities is a political act, involving as it does an unusual statement of intent to work with a minority group it is as easy to hate as it is to ignore. It is also a difficult act, as it brings us in close connection with a form of psychic chaos we wish to disavow. This work is messy and challenges our carefully constructed notions of boundary and neutrality. Patients' minds can be chaotic, unpredictable, and often deadening. Working with disability often lacks the excitement of working with those whose minds are fizzing with ideas, thoughts, and connections. It can sometimes be tedious in ways that can cause us to fear that our own minds may atrophy through disuse. People with intellectual disabilities occupy the lowest rungs of society's ladder for a complex interplay of reasons—not least of which is linked to our unconscious fears that close encounters with disability increase our own vulnerability to our minds losing their power. The more, then, that we can think about and process the immense power of encountering, working alongside, and with people with disabilities, the less likely we will be to perpetuate society's insidious process of disavowal, hatred, and fear.

## References

Abadiea, A., & Gayb, S. (2006). The impact of presumed consent legislation on cadaveric organ donation: a cross-country study. *Journal of Health Economics, 25*: 599–620.

Berg, J. W., & Appelbaum, P. S. (2001). *Informed Consent: Legal Theory and Clinical Practice*. New York: Oxford University Press.

Boyd, K. K. (1996). Power imbalances and therapy. *Focus, 11(9)*: 1–4.

Bybee, J., & Zigler, E. (1999). Outerdirectedness in individuals with and without mental retardation: a review. In: E. Zigler & D. Bennett-Gates (Eds.), *Personality Development in Individuals with Mental Retardation* (pp. 165–205). Cambridge: Cambridge University Press.

Clark, P. L. (1933). *The Nature and Treatment of Amentia*. London: Baillière, Tindall & Cox.

Corbett, A. (2009). Words as a second language: the psychotherapeutic challenge of severe disability. In: T. Cottis (Ed.), *Intellectual Disability, Trauma and Psychotherapy*. London: Routledge.

Corbett, A. (2012). Becoming the author: issues of consent, power and agency in the forensic assessment of people with intellectual disabilities. Centre for Professional Practice, Canterbury: University of Kent.

Dalla-Vorgia, P., Lascaratos, P., Skiadas, P., & Garanis-Papadatos, T. (2001). Is consent in medicine a concept only of modern times? *Journal of Medical Ethics, 27(1)*: 59–61.

Dickinson, K., Bunn, F., Wentz, R., Edwards. P., & Roberts, I. (2000). Size and quality of randomised controlled trials in head injury: review of published studies. *British Medical Journal, 320*: 1308–1311.

Freud, S. (1904a). Freud's psychoanalytic procedure. *SE. 7*: 247–254. London: Hogarth.

Gardner, H. (1983). *Frames of Mind: The Theory of Multiple Intelligences*. New York: Basic Books.

Gilbert, P. (2006). Social care services and the social perspective. *Psychiatry, 5(10)*: 341–345.

Gill, M. B. (2004). Presumed consent, autonomy, and organ donation. *Journal of Medicine and Philosophy, 29(1)*: 37–59.

Hinshelwood, R. D. (1991). Psychodynamic formulation in assessment for psychotherapy. *British Journal of Psychotherapy, 8(2)*: 166–174.

Hopper, E. (2012). Some challenges to the capacity to think, link and hope in the provision of psychotherapy for the learning disabled. In: J. Adlam, A. Aiyegbusi, P. Kleinot, A. Motz, & C. Scanlon (Eds.), *The Therapeutic Milieu Under Fire: Security and Insecurity in Forensic Mental Health*. London: Jessica Kingsley.

Jayyusi, L. (1984). *Categorization and the Moral Order*. London: Routledge.

Jensen, A. R. (1998). *The g Factor: The Science of Mental Ability*. Westport, CT: Praeger/Greenwood.

Katz, J. (2002). *The Silent World of Doctor and Patient*. Baltimore: John Hopkins University Press.

Kaufman, S. B., & Singer, J. L. (2004). Applying the theory of successful intelligence to psychotherapy training and practice. *Imagination, Cognition, and Personality, 23*: 325–355.

Kent, A. (2003). Consent and confidentiality in genetics: whose information is it anyway? *Journal of Medical Ethics, 29*: 16–18.

Kim, S. Y. H., Caine, E. D., Currier, G. W., Leibovici, A., & Ryan, J. M. (2001). Assessing the competence of persons with Alzheimer's disease in providing informed consent for participation in research. *American Journal of Psychiatry, 158*: 712–717.

Lane, M. S. (2007). *Method and Politics in Plato's Statesman*. Cambridge: Cambridge University Press.

Mayer, J. D., Salovey, P., & Caruso, D. R. (2000). Emotional intelligence. In: R. J. Sternberg (Ed.), *Handbook of Intelligence*. New York: Cambridge University Press.

Mead, G. H. (1934). *Mind, Self and Society*. Chicago, IL: University of Chicago Press.

Miller, F. P., Vandome, A. F., & McBrewster, J. (2009). *Informed Consent*. Mauritius: Alphascript Publishing.

Murdoch, S. (2009). *IQ: How Psychology Hijacked Intelligence*. London: Gerald Duckworth.

Murphy, G., & Clare, I. C. H. (2003). Adults' capacity to make legal decisions. In: D. Carson & R. Bull (Eds.), *Handbook of Psychology in Legal Contexts*. Chichester: Wiley.

Murphy, G., & O'Callaghan, A. (2004). Capacity of adults with intellectual disabilities to consent to sexual relationships. *Psychological Medicine, 34*: 1–11.

O'Driscoll, D. (2009). Psychotherapy and intellectual disability: a historical view. In: T. Cottis (Ed.), *Intellectual Disability, Trauma and Psychotherapy*. London: Routledge.

O'Neill, P. (1998). *Negotiating Consent in Psychotherapy*. New York: New York University Press.

Roberts, L. W., Geppert, C., McCarty, T., & Obenshain, S. S. (2003). Evaluating medical students' skills in obtaining informed consent for HIV testing. *Journal of General Internal Medicine, 18*: 112–119.

Salovey, P., & Mayer, J. D. (1990). Emotional intelligence. *Imagination, Cognition, and Personality, 9*: 185–211.

Schneider, C. E. (1998). *The Practice of Autonomy: Patients, Doctors, and Medical Decisions*. Oxford: Oxford University Press.

Schofield, W. (1964). *Psychotherapy: The Purchase of Friendship*. Englewood Cliffs, NJ: Prentice Hall.

Sinason, V. (1992). *Mental Handicap and the Human Condition: New Approaches from the Tavistock*. London: Free Association.

Sternberg, R. J. (1997). *Successful Intelligence*. New York: Plume.

Sternberg, R. J., & Detterman, D. K. (Eds.) (1986). *What Is Intelligence? Contemporary Viewpoints on Its Nature and Definition*. New Jersey: Ablex.

Strauman, T. J., & Higgins, E. T. (1987). Automatic activation of self-discrepancies and emotional syndromes: when cognitive structures influence affect. *Journal of Personality and Social Psychology, 53*: 1004–1014.

Symington, N. (1992). Countertransference with mentally handicapped clients. In: A. Waitman & S. Conboy-Hill (Eds.), *Psychotherapy and Mental Handicap*. London: Sage.

Whitaker, S. (2006). What's in a name? Alternatives to learning disability. *Mental Health and Learning Disabilities Research and Practice, 3*: 177–191.

Whitaker, S. (2008). Intellectual disability: a concept in need of revision? *British Journal of Developmental Disabilities, 54*: 3–9.

Wolfensberger, W. (1992). *A Brief Introduction to Social Role Valorization.* New York: Syracuse University.

Wong, J. G., Clare, I. C. H., Gunn, M. J., & Holland, A. J. (1999). Capacity to make health care decisions: its importance in clinical practice. *Psychological Medicine, 29(2):* 437–446.

# CHAPTER THREE

# Clinical snobbery—get me out of here! New clinical paradigms for children with complex disturbances

*Camila Batmanghelidjh*

## Introduction

Isabella is fourteen years old. Her behaviour is described as "savage"; she assaults other people, attacks the wall with her fists, slams her head into the concrete, and licks the blood that pours down her face.

Henry won't move from under a car. Wherever he goes, he finds the nearest car and crawls beneath it for shelter.

David is lethal: his personality is very disturbing. In conversation, he calls you "madam" or "sir" as if he is about to stab you with the razor-sharp rigidity of his fake politeness.

These young people are too high-risk to be treated in a clinical setting through one-to-one or group psychotherapy. Having acquired the label "hard to reach", they survive in the underbellies of our city, ducking and diving national hatred.

In the 1800s, the social reformer Mary Carpenter declared such behaviour the result of poor parental care. She didn't have brain-scanning machines or sophisticated psychological tools, but she observed that these children were different and required a comprehensive package of care: "These children have been hitherto so despised that they hardly know whether there is within them anything to be respected. They therefore feel no respect to others" (Carpenter, 1851, p. 83). Her remedy was to give them love, respect, and kindness.

As Carpenter protested in the Houses of Parliament against children being locked up, across the sea Freud was conceptualising his model of psychological well-being. In the cocoon of his consulting rooms, free-associating patients were facilitating pathways into the mind. Here, too, a decision was being made to develop interventions for those in need of help through talking.

The history of siloed packages of care is a perverse by-product of Cartesian thinking, where the mind and body are separated for attention. Not much has changed: therapeutic thinkers fight their philosophical corners—the Jungians, Kleinians, Freudians, gestalt psychologists, cognitive behaviourists. The menu is suffocatingly long, peppered with clinical self-righteousness as every framework claims supremacy. The fact is that many of these theoretical structures have more in common than they would like to admit and, on the whole, their constructs are conventional: two people in a room thinking and talking, with one holding the authoritative position while the other observes their position as patient. Those who don't abide by the conventions of these therapeutic contracts are described as "hard to reach", "not ready for therapy", or "incapable of mentalising". There is no room for Isabella, Henry, and David.

In this chapter, I will attempt to show the challenges faced by vulnerable children, young people, and their families, on a personal level and in the context of national statistics on childhood maltreatment. From the narratives, I hope to draw out central concerns and make clear why current therapeutic models fail to deliver solutions for clients with complex needs. Finally, I illustrate an alternative framework in which professionals collaborate with a view to creating service delivery models that have genuine impact. Ultimately, I ask the question: is clinical intellectual snobbery prohibiting effective work with those most in need?

## Getting to know the children and young people

As a psychotherapist, I have spent nearly thirty years working with vulnerable children. Most of my clinical practice has been in the community. It began with setting up a therapeutic provision for Women's Aid, where I saw children and women hugely impacted by domestic violence and further traumatised by depleted social-care interventions.

I also worked at Oxford Gardens, an NSPCC unit, where my work involved collaborating with a team responsible for assessing men who had sexually abused their own children. There, I acquired a profound understanding of the cyclical nature of child abuse, as I watched grown men break down into tears while recounting how they had been harmed as children.

Very early on, I learned that childhood maltreatment crosses economic and class divides. I met children who had been abused in some of the wealthiest homes in London: children who were being hit with belts, children whose mothers could barely attach to them, children who were being parented chaotically by the servants, children who, as young as three, were being put under intense pressure to pass entrance exams for top public schools.

At twenty-five, following six years of clinical practice, I was offered a part-time job as a psychotherapist in south London's family service units. My brief was to set up and deliver a therapeutic service for vulnerable children. As referrals arrived on my desk, I began to notice a pattern. Many of the children had been repeatedly referred to agencies but, following one or two clinic appointments, files would conclude with a "no-show" statement. Either the client was deemed unsuitable for therapy or the parent would not take the child to the sessions. Initially, I thought that collecting and delivering the children to sessions would solve this problem, but I soon realised the difficulty was lack of parental commitment. Children were never at home to be picked up or parents would disappear for hours, leaving me with children in the minibus who couldn't be dropped off after their sessions.

It was at this point that I met a seven-year-old girl. The referring educational psychologist anxiously described how this girl would put a plastic reading folder over her head and wrap a towel around her neck in the hope that she would suffocate. She had tried to jump in front of cars and throw herself off buildings. The local authority's biggest concern was that a suicide attempt would succeed on school premises. Realising that her mother would not be able to commit to bringing her to therapy, I decided to conduct our sessions in the school library with the suitcase of toys and art materials I had used in the houses of the rich (reluctant to take their children to NHS clinics for fear of being identified).

Working with this girl had a huge impact on my professional life. Our sessions were burdened by her profound and penetrating silence.

Veiled by a blonde fringe, her piercing blue eyes held my glance in a challenge as she drew bizarre pictures of babies' heads on gorilla bodies and birds' heads attached to children's limbs. I told her I felt something sinister was being shoved into me. She then disclosed that she had been sexually abused since the age of five by three men living in a tower block opposite her house.

As a young child, incapable of reproducing dates or sequences of events, she couldn't be the kind of witness the Crown Prosecution Service needed. The men were subsequently imprisoned after an older child brought allegations against them. As I watched the disclosure systems re-traumatise the little girl, I recognised profound flaws in the delivery of therapeutic provisions for vulnerable children. Most of the rigour exercised in relation to childhood maltreatment is connected to gathering evidence for prosecution. The provision of reparative care is patchy and chronically under-resourced, highlighting a wider cultural perversion: bias towards evidence-gathering and disclosure rather than therapeutic holding and reparation. Children perceive adults as trying to extract details of the abuse and discarding them after disclosure. Cleaning a broom cupboard in the seven-year-old's school, I wondered what to call a therapeutic service for children. That's how my first charity, Place2Be, was founded.

I was struck by the extraordinary dignity and fortitude with which vulnerable children negotiated their complex and often high-risk family settings. A ten-year-old boy whose mother was a sex-worker prevented himself from falling asleep to ensure his mother's clients didn't assault her. At approximately 4 a.m. he would have a nap and by 8 a.m. he was making his way to school. He was not dramatic. He did not exhibit disturbed behaviours. No one would have known how much risk he was negotiating had he not self-referred to Place2Be for therapeutic support.

Therapy services are beyond a child's reach unless an adult is sensitive to their difficulties and committed to attending appointments. Internationally, it is recognised that more than eighty per cent of child abuse is perpetuated by immediate family members and friends, who are likely to sabotage the path to help (May-Chahal & Cawson, 2005). It was the horror with which these children anticipated the school holidays that alerted me to their dependence on the school environment as a safety net and source of nourishment when, without school meals during the holidays, they would have minimal access to food. So, in 1996, I founded Kids Company. My original intention was to provide a service for vulnerable children during the school holidays to sustain their resilience.

As we set up our first centre beneath railway arches in Camberwell, we did not anticipate that, within weeks, about a hundred boys from local gangs would come to terrorise us. None of the theoretically rich courses in the therapy schools of Hampstead had prepared us for these knife-wielding, substance-abusing, intensely criminalised, and intimidating adolescent boys. I was out of my depth, profoundly disempowered and paralysed, as my so-called posh vocabulary and their street-talk polarised us. The bridge was created by my Persian culture and its emphasis on good hospitality. No matter how violent the boys were, I greeted them with courtesy and welcomed them as guests. For their part, they were deeply curious about my refusal to retaliate.

Paradoxically, we were brought together through compassionate companionship. They helped me and my team understand their world, and I offered them a framework through which they could begin to consider their traumas rather than embodying them through the compulsion to repeat. Before long, we had four hundred children in the railway arches, including some of the most sought-after south London criminals and Oliver Twist lookalikes under ten who spent their days avoiding their parents' drug-fuelled rages while scavenging in the bins for food. Within two years, I had in my heart the intimate life narratives of these kids who, I discovered, were neither random nor bizarre in their disturbed behaviours.

As they recounted horrifically humiliating events, they confided that they struggled to calm down and, at times, used violence to achieve post-assault soothing. Evacuation of tension was their substitute maternal experience. I used to go home at night and wonder why so many children described an inability to calm down. It was this consistency that set me to find scientists who could acknowledge the children's experiences beyond the platitudes of "young offenders and delinquents".

With support from the Royal Society of Medicine, Kids Company facilitated a symposium of experts. From it emerged our "Peace of Mind" campaign (www.kidspeaceofmind.org), where scientists conducted research based on the narratives shared by the children. Sixteen years later, shocking data are emerging. One in five of the children who initially turned to Kids Company's educational facility, the Urban Academy, had been shot at and/or stabbed. One in four had immediate family members shot at or stabbed. Child sexual abuse was thirteen times more prevalent compared to controls. Severe to extreme levels of emotional neglect were fifteen times greater. Exposure to different types of violence was eleven times greater, with the children having, cumulatively, more than two incidents of abuse (physical, sexual, emotional, and/or neglect), thirteen times more than controls (Cecil et al., 2012).

In a separate piece of research carried out by Queen Mary University of London from 2005 to 2008 (Gaskell, 2008), eighty-four per cent of the children who came to Kids Company's street-level centres arrived homeless, eighty-seven per cent presented with complex emotional and psychiatric disorders, eighty-one per cent were criminally involved at the point of self-referral, eighty-two per cent were addicted to substances, and ninety-one per cent were not in education or employment. Independent consultants demonstrated that one-third of the children accessing the street-level centres didn't have beds, one-third wanted to run away from home, more than half had sleeping problems, and eighteen per cent didn't possess a single pair of underpants (Hillman, 2012; unpublished correspondence).

Children and young people hear about Kids Company services at street level or in the forty schools where we provide services. Initially, they come asking for basic provisions, such as food and somewhere to live. Once they trust us, their life stories are shared, and we're invited into their homes, where we often find equally depleted younger children. Our teams regularly remove human and animal faeces from bedrooms and find rats in the fridge. Feeling rage towards their carers is too easy. They are best described as survivors: in living together, both adult and child are attempting to endure trauma rather than thriving together in a shared, stable, and loving environment.

Kids Company's services have evolved over time. Our provision can best be described as a substitute parental function, addressing children's needs across education, physical and mental health, social care, employment, and personal development.

Before describing the children's psychological states and the proposed therapeutic model, I'd like to contextualise numbers and levels of need. There is a fundamental discrepancy between what is recognised by the UK government and the scale of childhood maltreatment identified by international researchers. According to Unicef (2007), there are at least 1.5 million children being maltreated in Britain every year and we are bottom of the league of twenty-one wealthiest countries in the world for child well-being. One in ten of those under sixteen has mental health difficulties (Green et al., 2005), and approximately one million young people are unemployed (Parliamentary Briefing Papers, 2013), many of them not in education. It is estimated that 3.5 million children are living with substance-abusing parents (Addaction, 2012), while around 1.75 million children live in workless households (ONS, 2012). The average age at which girls start prostitution in Britain is twelve (Home Office, 2004).

Analysis of child protection figures over the past eleven years demonstrates that, on average, some 612,000 children are referred to child protection services every year. However, the majority are filtered through an assessment process, with 42,330 children ending up on the child protection register. Similar numbers are de-registered annually, but an average of twenty-six per cent of these children go back on the register within the year, indicating they were prematurely removed (DfE, 2011).

In practice, these statistics translate as depleted social work departments with mind-bogglingly high and often unethical intake thresholds. Imagine deciding that your department will accept children who have been physically abused with an implement but not those assaulted without an implement. The Rochdale case, involving the sexual abuse of young girls, demonstrated that social work and police departments considered fifteen-year-old girls' involvement in prostitution to be a "lifestyle choice".

Unfortunately, as professionals feel unable to transform conditions for vulnerable children, perverse strategies develop to defend against demand and minimise personal shame, as those wanting to help children cannot deliver that help. What civilised world decides to leave a ten-year-old boy with drug-addicted parents while taking his little brother into care, because the ten-year-old can shoplift food to survive while the two-year-old can't? Privately, politicians admit that children's social care is not fit for purpose, but none of them want to go near it: the rot is too profound and the gains for addressing it too minimal. Children don't vote, so they can't hold politicians accountable.

It is in this context that Isabella, Henry, and David negotiate their invisible citizenship.

Isabella, aged ten, was raped in the family home by her father, following a prolonged period of bullying, assault, and violation. Isabella's mother was sexually abused by her stepfather and manages the trauma through disassociation. Home became profoundly unsafe for Isabella and she took to the streets. She describes how, aged eleven, she stood trapped in a public toilet as thirty men came in to have sex with her. Too disturbed to manage in school, she was permanently excluded at twelve. Between the ages of twelve and fourteen, she spent every day being taken around the brothels of London by pimps. She sat opposite me and matter-of-factly said that she'd had sex with more than two hundred men, among them two significantly older men who became substitute parental figures, as her mother had never tried to find her. Social services did not know that an underage girl was being chronically violated. Isabella barely attended school between the ages of eleven and fourteen. She presents as unkempt. She has contracted sexually transmitted diseases. She self-harms.

Henry is a slight boy, with translucent skin and dark circles under his eyes. He hasn't been battered. The pain he feels is about being insignificant. He experiences himself as not being cared for. No one cooks for him, spends time with him, or wonders what he's thinking or feeling. The only time he is noticed is when arguments erupt in the house and he is ferociously shouted at while trying, in vain, to calm down his warring parents. He likes to hide, wherever he is. His favourite space is the underbelly of a car. Henry refuses to eat and is emaciated. A home visit reveals that he doesn't even have a bed; he has squashed several cardboard boxes on top of each other to generate a cushion against the concrete floor.

David was sexually abused by his older brother. His mother was cruel, administering bizarre punishments and frequently assaulting him with belts, sticks, and electricity cables. He can't sustain engagement in any setting. He presents as capable and hardworking at first. Then, when he feels he's being ignored, his whole system collapses into self-loathing, after which he disengages, never to return. He can't sleep and admits to having stabbed many people. He feels scared of himself because he knows that, enraged, he can turn into a lethal killer. So he tries to avoid conflict by withdrawing from all group settings for fear that he may "switch". David's biggest fear is that he will kill the drug users who shelter on the stairwell outside his flat. He can't go to sleep because he's a member of a notorious Brixton gang and fears the Peckham rivals who have spotted him walking home.

## Repercussions of childhood maltreatment

The biggest challenge in understanding the repercussions of childhood maltreatment is in the separation of social, biological, and cognitive concerns, reflecting administrative divisions in public management. As government departments are divided, so children's needs are chopped up to match. Health deals with mental and physical issues, social services tackle social care, criminal justice addresses offending behaviours, and education educates. The adults involved in running these disparate departments struggle to communicate, so children don't stand a chance of understanding the help construct and how to access it. For "lone children", children who don't have a functioning carer in their lives, there is no grown-up navigating the path to help.

Central government has a vacuous approach to the care of children and, on the whole, tends to prioritise education. Social care is the "ugly sister" who has to be attended to but can't be prioritised. Consequently, historically, the weakest ministers have held the brief for children's social care. An analysis of government policy over the years demonstrates poverty of vision and aspiration for the most vulnerable children in our communities and chronic under-investment in children's welfare services.

The consequence of the national blind spot for childhood vulnerability is a sense of profound shame. Children who have been violated experience a catastrophic loss of dignity, which has, at its heart, the notion of unlovability. They often explain away the harm they've endured as a consequence of being, fundamentally, too flawed to be chosen for love. An intrinsic sense of the self as damaged and disgusting develops. So much time is spent hiding the self for fear that personal shame will become public and result in the group's collective rejection, mutually and publicly acknowledging the hidden disgusting self.

The active abuse of children, combined with their passive neglect, results in a damaged sense of self and a fear of public judgement. Our most humiliated children and young people are rejected again when they turn to our helping agencies. As workers are too under-resourced to transform, they perceive their incapacity as evidence of personal failure and endeavour to hide their shame from onlookers to avoid humiliation. When a shamed worker and a shamed child come face to face, in the refusing glance of both, the acid of humiliation is generated, rupturing the care contract. At a very basic yet profound level, the primary need of an individual who has been harmed is to be welcomed and cherished.

Repeated negative experiences of care result in children developing a sarcastic and avoidant or hopeless attitude towards agencies, setting up a paradoxical interaction whereby help-seeking behaviours are sabotaged by defensive, avoidant behaviours. An under-resourced workforce driven by targets and time limits engages in an emotional economy where help is delivered to those who produce the best results and complex cases are made to disappear.

Neuroscience is giving us a greater understanding of the multi-dimensional challenges faced by our most vulnerable children. As a result of advancements in the fields of neuroimaging and epigenetics, we're beginning to understand the complex pathways involved in brain development. The brain is the object of the mind, while the person is the subject. In the context of a rapidly evolving science, we're realising that the period of adolescence in human infants doesn't arrive at full biological maturity until the age of about thirty (Lebel & Beaulieu, 2011).

The brain's more primitive and emotionally driven areas, the limbic system situated deep inside the brain, develop much earlier than the pre-frontal cortex situated closer to the skull. Growth is bottom up, resulting in primitive and emotional material dominating the pro-social and regulatory functions of the pre-frontal cortex (Panksepp, 1998). We also know that neurons are continuously developing, pruning themselves and developing stronger connections through myelination, the process of white matter building up around a neuron. As the brain develops towards maturity, it has less grey matter (neurons) but more white matter (myelination), making neuronal functioning more efficient in transmitting chemical and electrical messages and connections. A healthy adult develops more efficient and economical brain functioning using the best and most rapid pathways (Jernigan et al., 2011; Paus et al., 2001).

Childhood maltreatment, both active abuse and neglect, results in structural and functional assault on the brain, generating consequences that significantly affect how an individual processes cognition, generates resilience, and regulates emotion and energy. Simply put, childhood maltreatment creates inefficiencies in brain functioning and, as a result, delivers a cascade of negative consequences in neuronal and physiological development. For the maltreated child, these consequences can emerge across physiological, cognitive, and personality systems (Dannlowski et al., 2012; Twardosz & Lutzker, 2010; Walker, McMillan, & Mittal, 2007).

Maltreated children describe hyper-agitation, depression, disassociation, night terrors, a propensity to explode with anger, exceptional lethargy, feelings of disconnectedness, inability to organise perceptions, and suicidality. In employment and educational settings, they describe finding it difficult to obey rules, as any form of order is interpreted as negative control, like an abuser's command to harm. They often describe struggling with a sense of time, as historic abuse is brought to life by events and characteristics that contain similarities with the past and trigger emotional responses related to harm.

High levels of anxiety make learning challenging (Veltman & Browne, 2012), as instructions are not taken in or not retained. A general sense of confusion, and the arbitrariness of the world as experienced by those who have been harmed, mean that a belief in organisation and endeavour is not sustained. Catastrophic meaninglessness often shadows victims of abuse. Their notions of order have been shattered, making it hard to believe that systematic and sustained effort will lead to good outcomes and rewards. When dreams are perceived as delusions, pursuing a future becomes pointless.

On a physical level, as children are terrorised, overexposure to fright hormones propels the body into a chronic stress response, impacting all the main organs and the cells of the body, where the narrative of abuse cannot be found but its emotional legacy remains painfully vivid (Cicchetti & Rogosch, 2001a; Dedovic et al., 2009). Autoimmune disorders, digestive disorders, hormonal dysregulation, premature ageing, and inflammatory diseases have all been linked to the repercussions of childhood maltreatment (Danese et al., 2007; Dube et al., 2009; Garner & Shonkoff, 2012; Shalev et al., 2012).

Child abuse dysregulates the human system in a comprehensive and complex way (Rogosch et al., 2011). Body and mind cannot be separated. The damage is environmentally driven, which means, if the vicious cycle of child abuse is to be protected against, the social conditions children negotiate have to be addressed simultaneously (Belsky, Conger, & Capaldi, 2009; Caspi & Moffit, 2006; Wong et al., 2010).

It would be wrong to say that children recover from maltreatment. However, we can help children to acquire mastery over their trauma rather than be mastered by it. It is this transition from experiencing the reaction to viewing the reaction those who conceptualise mentalisation hope to arrive at. The ability to mentalise is synonymous with having a sense of personal agency, whether that means thinking about the thoughts we're having or making a decision about a deed that needs to be carried out (Fonagy et al., 2004). The premise is that the individual will sustain sufficient calm to allow the mature part to exercise protection over the more vulnerable part.

Our abilities to self-soothe and self-care are primarily given to us through the attachment relationships we have been exposed to. A baby is profoundly reliant on its carers. In appropriate and well-attuned responses, parental caregivers help the child to develop a personal vocabulary for internal and interpersonal states, as well as personal strategies to modify and regulate these states. It is in this context that the quality of parental attachments is so important, giving children the resilience to meet and overcome adversity (Sroufe et al., 1999).

Children who have had poor care sustain a diminished personal repertoire in managing emotional states. When their system is further challenged by traumatic assaults, they are more likely to become over-whelmed and catastrophically disempowered. Post-traumatic stress disorder is a complex consequence of this disempowerment, whereby trauma masters the self rather than the self mastering the trauma. As the potency of the self is diminished, the trauma grows accumulatively, adding injury to injury, and eroding the potency of the child to the point where despair permeates and the child feels doubly assaulted—by what happened and by the consequence of the traumatic event (Schore, 2002).

Those who have had good attachments are thought to internalise the caregiver's strategies, eventually owning the function and being able to use it to protect against adversity. The grown-up needed by the baby becomes the grown-up within, managing personal vulnerabilities and making decisions about personal growth. If sustained quality attachment is the route to facilitating mentalisation, the fundamental thera-peutic task for those who have endured childhood maltreatment is one of a re-parenting opportunity with all that is involved.

Good parents do everything to promote the growth of their chil-dren. They address physical, emotional, social, and educational needs in recognition of human development being a complex interdependent system. The primary crisis of maltreated children and young people is a premature assault on their sense of personal care. The trauma is bigger than the child's ability to manage it appropriately. Feeling overpow-ered, the child is plunged into catastrophic loneliness, ruptured from a social network that could potentially afford them resilience. One ther-apy session per week, if you're lucky enough to get it, is not enough to deliver reparation. Neither is a social work visit or access to education.

Traumatised children need an intensive multisystemic package of care, with the emotional drivers attributed to parental nurture at the heart of its philosophy.

The scale of the problem is too big for all maltreated children to be taken into local authority care. Outcomes from current care structures are poor, with disturbed children frustrating foster carers and often continually excluded from care settings (Stein, 2006). Repeated re-traumatisation due to precarious social-care settings results in children being continuously set back in recovery. A therapeutic model with the robustness and sophistication to take on board and deal with the multiple repercussions of childhood maltreatment is needed.

## Proposed therapeutic paradigm for complex trauma

In the past thirty years, while working with vulnerable children, my team and I have had the privilege of learning from them how to create an effective therapeutic service. Kids Company ended up piloting a community psychosocial intervention with a two-tiered delivery point. In creating our Schools Programme, we placed a multidisciplinary team of workers supported by diverse volunteers in schools. Beautiful playrooms have been created with toys and art materials. Children are collected from class and taken to their sessions for therapeutic support, while social workers, occupational therapists, and health workers address the whole family's needs where appropriate and liaise with external agencies on behalf of the child.

The child is Kids Company's primary client. Parents, carers, and teachers are considered secondary clients, whose needs are met provided they correspond with the child's. While therapeutic reparations are delivered, a team of artists, musicians, performers, sports workers, and inspirational volunteers generate a menu of possible experiences for each child in the school setting, enhancing and diversifying aspirations while generating joy, which contributes to the child's sense of resilience and hopefulness.

Any child in need of greater help is encouraged to access Kids Company's street-level centres local to their neighbourhood. Multidisciplinary staff teams are available from morning until ten at night, after which an emergency team is available on the phone if children require immediate assistance. Psychiatrists, educational psychologists, teachers, doctors, nurses, youth workers, complementary health professionals, artists, cooks, security guards, musicians, sports workers, and volunteers unite, with everyone's professional skills seen as equally important and necessary to the community.

The street-level centres are decorated beautifully. Research by Professor Alessandra Lemma of Tavistock and Portman NHS Trust reveals that the children who access our services first become attached to the fabric of the building and its routine: the environment is the primary source of attachment as a "mother brick". The children go on to extend their attachments to multiple staff and then narrow them down to keyworkers with whom they develop deeper attachments (Lemma, 2010).

We provide three meals a day, alongside education, fun activities, employment, housing, health, and aspirational advice. Children are given individual keyworkers but learn to attach to a diverse range of carers, whose care function is united under the umbrella of Kids Company. Children and young people not in school and surviving through the criminal network self-refer to these centres and are helped to leave the streets because they're offered a realistic and appealing alternative.

The syllabus of recovery and reparation in our centres is driven by a systemic tackling of the repercussions of complex trauma. In addressing economic deficiencies, children are made safe and given shelter. Dysregulated physiological states are addressed through complementary health treatments, medical interventions where necessary, and provision of regular nourishment. Staff members enhance the ability of the children to mentalise their physical and emotional states and use strategies to master overwhelming feelings and physiological reactions. Protection, routine, verbalisation, practice of care, aspirations, and educational pathways to achieving in the world of work enable the children to grow into valuing and valued citizens.

The realities of challenging neighbourhoods deliver further blows, and children are helped to negotiate setbacks without becoming demoralised. This systematic and multidisciplinary care model has aspects of many disparate theoretical frameworks. In its sustained daily delivery, it mimics the consistency of psychoanalysis. In being solution-driven, it adopts much of the cognitive, analytic, solution-focused therapies. In promoting unconditional positive regard, it generates the therapeutic contract at the core of person-centred therapy. In using the arts, aspirationally and therapeutically, it adopts many of the practical interventions conceptualised by the arts therapies. By having a multisystemic delivery point, aspects of principles of family therapy gestalt and psychodynamic frameworks of care are realised. Physical repercussions of trauma are addressed simultaneously, while health-promoting activities are facilitated. Children and young people are helped to reframe their life narratives in order to sustain a drive towards achievement without being paralysed by the sabotaging drivers of traumatic memories. Above all, a rejected child feels welcomed, cherished, and embraced by a community which mimics the challenges of family settings while simultaneously affording resilience (Lemma, 2010).

Independent research over the past sixteen years has demonstrated that this is a highly effective model in delivering outcomes and personal reparation (Gaskell, 2008). Results have shown efficacy levels above eighty-five per cent in returning children and young people to education and employment. Reading ages have consistently gone up. Young people have achieved at university, many going on to Oxford, Cambridge, and other Russell Group universities. Nurses, ambulance drivers, accountants, bankers, arts and IT workers, social workers, and teachers are among the graduates of Kids Company. But it has taken consistent, everyday care, addressing challenges across health, emotional well-being, education, and social care to achieve results.

Some young people have gone on to develop mental illnesses, but even those who ended up in prison described being less perverse and having more ability to parent their own children appropriately because they'd gone through this community reparation.

In view of the model working so well, why isn't it adopted more widely? Traumatised children have an uncanny ability to face the truth. Conventional and prohibitive boundaries are crossed during abuse, but this can also lead to a more creative outlook. In this context, paradoxically, while the system is assaulted and plunged into defensive survival, other aspects of cognition develop more profound freedoms. The mind becomes capable of thinking beyond boundaries. In a very simple way, the children of Kids Company told us what worked in helping them achieve mastery over their trauma. We listened and attempted to deliver.

A response that has been incubated in some of the most depleted communities struggles to achieve replication in the mainstream because professionals are too bound to singular theoretical frameworks, often fighting to hold on to therapeutic models, as if rigid adherence to a singular philosophy is guaranteed to deliver quality. Furthermore, there is a reticence to cross boundaries in the belief that thought and talking should be separated from the body and that the body should be separated from its social environment. In siloed intellectual frames, we chop up human beings into fragmented pieces while deluding ourselves that we're making them whole.

## The challenge ahead

Undoubtedly, maltreated children display enormous courage. It would be so much easier to remain hopeless when hopefulness can be so painful and disappointing. Yet, given appropriate help, the majority of children who have been harmed can make progress. They have the courage to change and to embrace what works. It is by following their example that workers attempting to deliver solutions need to find their own moral compass and the bravery to follow its direction.

There is a discrepancy between what clinicians privately believe delivers recovery and what they're publicly prepared to admit. In the privacy of their homes, away from their colleagues, they might describe kindness, generosity, practical resources, encouragement, affection, welcome, patience, curiosity, delight, checking of envy and pride as being some of the most effective ingredients of therapeutic encounters. But professionals can sometimes struggle to retain the truth of their feelings once they get into the public space. Collectively, and often collusively, they define their functions and actions in the context of their clinical training, overemphasising intellectuality over humaneness as the potency of the reparation. They do this because the intellectualisation of care has evolved into snobbery, leading professionals to hide their humanity for fear of being ridiculed or perceived as unboundaried. The very people who are supposed to conceptualise the most effective care structures are the people who don't have the courage to do it for fear of being rejected. In the process, they reject children, who find their delivery models unreachable.

Fundamentally, good therapy is about a compassionate companionship: a whole human being helping another across all needs to achieve integration and the recipient, being empowered, recycling the compassionate moment. In the passing on of help, a community is generated and sustained. Whether traumatised or not, all human beings seek reciprocity and are devastated by alienation.

The question is: can the therapeutic community exercise enough bravery to go beyond clinical snobbery and generate more meaningful care paradigms for children and young people who are waiting to be restored to dignity? As one of the Kids Company children put it:

> Without a family you would be alone in the world, and it's such a big world, and such a little amount of you. (Kane, aged thirteen)

> No-one can tell but those who have witnessed it, the responsive love which is awakened in the heart of one of these forsaken ones by a kind look or word, or the purifying effect of the feeling, for many experienced for the first time, that they are "loved for themselves". (Carpenter, 1851, p. 74)

## References

Addaction (2012). *Breaking the Cycle: A Better Future for Families*. London: Addaction.

Belsky, J., Conger, R., & Capaldi, D. (2009). The intergenerational transmission of parenting: introduction to the special section. *Developmental Psychology, 45(5)*: 1201–1204.

Carpenter, M. (1851). *Reformatory Schools: For the Children of the Perishing and Dangerous Classes and for Juvenile Offenders*. London: Gilpin.

Caspi, A., & Moffitt, T. (2006). Gene—environment interactions in psychiatry: joining forces with neuroscience. *Neuroscience, 7(7)*: 583–590.

Cecil, C., McCrory, E., & Viding, E. (2012). *Neurocognitive Correlates of Developmental Adversity: Differences in Baseline Functioning and Response to Therapeutic Intervention*. In Progress: University College London.

Cicchetti, D., & Rogosch, F. A. (2001). The impact of child maltreatment and psychopathology on neuroendocrine functioning. *Development and Psychopathology, 13*: 783–804.

Danese, A., Pariante, C. M., Caspi, A., Taylor, A., & Poulton, R. (2007). Childhood maltreatment predicts adult inflammation in a life-course study. *Proceeding of the National Academy of Sciences USA, 104*: 1319–1324.

Dannlowski, U., Stuhrmann, A., Beutelmann, V., Zwanzger, P., Lenzen, T., Grotegerd, D., Domschke, K., Hohoff, C., Ohrmann, P., Bauer, J., Lindner, C., Postert, C., Konrad, C., Arolt, V., Heindel, W., Suslow, T., & Kugel, H. (2012). Limbic scars: long-term consequences of childhood maltreatment revealed by functional and structural magnetic resonance imaging. *Biological Psychiatry, 71(4)*: 286–293.

Dedovic, K., Duchesne, A., Andrews, J., Engert, V., & Pruessner, J. (2009). The brain and the stress axis: the neural correlates of cortisol regulation in response to stress. *NeuroImage, 47(3)*: 864–871.

Department for Education (2011). Characteristics of Children in Need in England, 2010–2011. At: www.education.gov.uk/rsgateway/DB/STR/d001041/index.shtml (accessed on 25 September 2013).

Dube, S. R., Fairweather, D., Pearson, W. S., Felitti, V. J., Anda, R. F., & Croft, J. B. (2009). Cumulative childhood stress and autoimmune diseases in adults. *Psychosomatic Medicine, 2(71)*: 243–250.

Fonagy, P., Gergely, G., Jurist, E., & Target, M. (2004). *Affect Regulation, Mentalization, and the Development of Self*. London: Karnac.

Garner, A. S., & Shonkoff, J. P. (2012). Early childhood adversity, toxic stress, and the role of the paediatrician: translating developmental science into lifelong health. *Pediatrics, 129(1)*: e224–e231.

Gaskell, C. (2008). *Kids Company Help with the Whole Problem: Evaluation of Kids Company*. London: Queen Mary University.

Green, H., McGinnity, A., & Meltzer, H. (2005). *Mental Health of Children and Young People in Great Britain*. London: Palgrave.

Home Office (2004). *Paying the price. A consultation paper on prostitution*. London: Home Office.

Jernigan, T., Baaré, W., Stiles, J., & Madsen, K. S. (2011). Postnatal brain development: structural imaging of dynamic neurodevelopmental processes. In: O. Braddick, J. Atkinson, & G. Innocenti (Eds.), *Progress in Brain Research, 189*: 77–92.

Lebel, C., & Beaulieu, C. (2011). Longitudinal development of human brain wiring continues from childhood into adulthood. *Journal of Neuroscience, 31(30)*: 10937–10947.

Lemma, A. (2010). The power of relationship: a study of key working as an intervention with traumatised young people. *Journal of Social Work Practice, 24(4)*: 409–427.

May-Chahal, C., & Cawson, P. (2005). Measuring child maltreatment in the United Kingdom: a study of the prevalence of child abuse and neglect. *Child Abuse and Neglect, 29(9)*: 969–984.

Office for National Statistics (2012). Statistical bulletin: working and workless households. At: www.ons.gov.uk/ons/rel/lmac/working-and-workless-households/2012/stb-working-and-workless-households-2012.html#tab-Children (accessed on 14 August 2013).

Panksepp, J. (1998). *Affective Neuroscience: The Foundations of Human and Animal Emotions*. New York: Oxford University Press.

Parlimentary Briefing Papers (2013). http://www. parliament. uk/briefing-papers/SN05871 (accessed on 14 August 2013).

Paus, T., Collins, D. L., Evans, A. C., Leonard, G., Pike, B., & Zijdenbos, A. (2001). Maturation of white matter in the human brain: a review of magnetic resonance studies. *Brain Research Bulletin, 54(3)*: 255–266.

Rogosch, F. A., Dackis, M. N., & Cicchetti, D. (2011). Child maltreatment and allostatic load: consequences for physical and mental health in children from low-income families. *Development and Psychopathology, 23*: 1107–1124.

Schore, A. (2002). Dysregulation of the right brain: a fundamental mechanism of traumatic attachment and the psychopathogenesis of post-traumatic stress disorder. *Australian and New Zealand Journal of Psychiatry, 36*: 9–30.

Shalev, I., Moffitt, T. E., Sugden, K., Williams, B., Houts, R. M., & Danese, A. (2013). Exposure to violence during childhood is associated with telomere erosion from 5 to 10 years of age: a longitudinal study. *Molecular Psychiatry, 18*: 576–581.

Sroufe, A., Carlson, E., Levy, A., & Egeland, B. (1999). Implications of attachment theory for developmental psychopathology. *Development and Psychopathology, 11(1)*: 1–13.

Stein, M. (2006). Research review: young people leaving care. *Child and Family Social Work, 11*: 273–279.

Twardosz, S., & Lutzker, J. R. (2010). Child maltreatment and the developing brain: a review of neuroscience perspectives. *Aggression and Violent Behaviour, 15(1)*: 59–68.

UNICEF (2007). *Report Card No. 7, Child Poverty in Perspective: An Overview of Child Well-Being in Rich Countries*. Florence: UNICEF.

Veltman, M., & Browne, D. (2012). Three decades of child maltreatment research: implications for the school years. *Trauma, Violence, Abuse, 2(3)*: 215–239.

Walker, F., McMillan, A., & Mittal, V. (2007). Adolescent psychopathology and the developing brain. In: *Neurohormones, Neurodevelopment and the Prodrome of Psychosis in Adolescence*. New York: Oxford University Press.

Wong, C. C., Caspi, A., Williams, B., Craig, I. W., Houts, R., Ambler, A., Moffitt, T. E., & Mill, J. (2010). A longitudinal study of epigenetic variation in twins. *Epigenetics, 5(6)*: 516–526.

# CHAPTER FOUR

# Why aren't we educating?
# Psychotherapy, psy-culture,
# and the psy-ber world

*Alison Bryan*

## Definitions

In this chapter, "psychoanalysis" and "psychotherapy" will be used interchangeably, to highlight the importance of contemporary psychoanalytic thinking, whether undertaken by an analyst or a psychotherapist. Perceptions of clinical differences between these modalities are acknowledged. The term "psychoanalysis" is equally understood as a theory through which to think about subjectivity, with political and social implications.

## Introduction

Psychoanalysis, Sass (1992, p. 20) argues, "is by far the most influential contemporary vision of human nature", but much of the peculiarities, inherent demands, and values of the psychoanalytic process are currently being lost from view within a world where the discourses surrounding therapeutic culture have led to an obfuscation of this foundational practice. Frosh (1991, p. 1) notes that "psychoanalysis has never had more to say about contemporary culture than it has now. On the whole, however, it is not psychoanalysts who are saying it." Yet the core concepts of psychoanalysis have contributed to and constructed the root systems upon which the current therapeutic diaspora flourishes. To this day, psychoanalysis and its closest relatives psychoanalytic and psychodynamic psychotherapy continue to provide a distinctive and relevant mode of treatment—although their tenets of the existence of an unconscious and how its existence may be observed in the therapeutic relationship are under threat.

Psychoanalysis, and derivative versions of analytic thinking in clinical practice, provide a means for the contemporary subject through which to make sense of their subjectivity, in a century when politics has become indisputably personal. The process of individualisation is linked to contemporary therapeutic culture in which, Lasch (1991) claims, our current hunger is for personal well-being, health, and psychic security. This chapter examines how psychoanalytic thinking and theory is an evident and relevant part of psy culture in the Western sociological landscape of the twenty-first century. It evaluates anti- and pro-therapy literature, and asks questions about the failure of psychotherapy to communicate its knowledge and relevance with conviction.

In this context, the terms "psychoanalysis" and "psychotherapy" refer to a subjective treatment mode conducted between the psychotherapist or analyst and client, within a carefully constructed and conducted therapeutic frame, most commonly on an open-ended basis, and usually for many months or more commonly years. It is a process that acknowledges its roots in the psychoanalytic theory articulated by Freud and subsequently taken forward by Klein, Bion, Winnicott, and others. It proposed a tenet of a dynamic unconscious which encompasses drives, phantasies, and primitive anxieties, held back from the conscious by repression. It acknowledges the concepts of defence mechanisms and transference neurosis, leading to behaviours whose meaning are unknown to the client at a conscious level. The unconscious, which can come forward through free association, encompasses both subversive and desiring forces which may prevent or bring about the actualisation of the subject. Psychoanalysis enters this unstable world aiming to release an "I", that may no longer perpetuate its sufferings but strive despite them. Psychoanalysis therefore holds considerable meaning beyond its clinical application, as a discourse with extensive influence within the subjects of linguistics, anthropology, history, archaeology, neurology, feminism, and psychology—without starting on religion. Under critique, the psychoanalytic theory of subjectivity thus presents either freedom for the subject, or an ambivalent means of subjugation.

## Current confusions

Freud's call to consider the potential of the "talking cure" (Breuer & Freud, 1893) has never been silenced. An indisputable starting point—and perhaps now, a return to home is called for. Psychoanalytic practice has become an endangered species, under threat by its own offspring. First, our genealogical progression has led, not so much as to a readable family tree, but to something more akin to a bramble bush. An enticing "Find a Therapist" button takes aspiring analysands, clients, or patients, into a thorny negotiation without protective gloves or a dictionary. Many have been lost, or have had scrapes in this briar. Further confusion arises around the position of psychotherapy in the lexicon of "psych" practices (psychiatrist, psychologist, psychoanalyst, psychotherapist, psychodynamics, and so on) which befuddle the lay person. And there is an additional red herring with the term "therapy" being attached to all manner of feel-good activities as a permission ticket, leading to questions being raised in general culture as to how to evaluate one therapy from another. As a result, clarity of profession for the clinical practitioner or process for the client is subtly undermined. To add to this sense of being squeezed, psychotherapy, at least within contemporary public services, is being offered salvation through three questionable means—the justification of evidence-based practice, the sanitisation of being medicalised, and legitimisation through partnership with cognitive behavioural therapy. In short, a home in scientism.

## Societal contexts

The psychoanalytic tenets of drives and defences listed above may already have a ring of the old-fashioned about them, but their continued significance is evident in contemporary sociological science, which maps the movement of the human being from a purely "moral subject of habit" (Rose, 1999, p. xviii) via "one of solidarity and citizen rights of the first half of the twentieth century, to the autonomous subject of choice and self-realisation as the twentieth century drew to a close" (Rose, 1999, intro). Referring to the significance of language in the construction and transformation of personhood, Rose points out that the growing practices of explaining ourselves in psychological terms and narratives leads to a necessarily new form of self-understanding. He goes as far as proposing that psychological systems now present a Foucauldian form of ethics, since these new procedures provide injunctions, prohibitions, and judgements with regards to how people conduct themselves.

Foucault's (1979) theory of the "disciplinary society" points to the ways in which each historical epoch produces technologies for control. These technologies are based on differentiations and particularly lean towards a "dividing practice" of duality around good–bad, or perhaps normal–pathological. Foucault expressed concern that psychoanalysis might be understood not as a fixed entity with authority on mental health or otherwise, but as one example, in perpetual flux, of bio-technico-power. This term refers to the ways in which systems of classification and forms of expertise might appear to be in the interest of an individual or a population, but are in fact new and further ways of governing them. He disliked psychoanalysis' claim to have knowledge of a subject's past since he believed that the subject is historically contingent with a changeable identity. Foucault saw danger in the normalisation of the subject in psychoanalysis and the ways in which the population might be categorised through it.

A broader expansion of this theme is taken up by Rose (1999) in *Governing the Soul*. Rose's central thesis is that cultures give rise to their own and specific technologies of the self, and that, in Western societies, we have a currently prevailing culture of "psy discourses". He places the therapeutic discourse within political neo-liberalism, which has commercial enterprise at its heart. Enterprise not only achieves economic strength, but a way of structuring the life of individuals, making them "entrepreneurs of themselves" where the "political subject is now less a social citizen with power and obligations deriving from membership of a collective body, than an individual whose citizenship is to be manifested through the free exercise of personal choice among a variety of marketed options" (1999, p. 230). The "techniques of psychotherapeutics" are bound to this injunction to selfhood, and sought by individuals who feel unable to bear the obligations of it. With full Foucauldian flavour, Rose sees psychotherapies as finding their meaning in restoring individuals to the capacity to function autonomously in this "contractual society of the self". However, through therapy, the self, as an economic unit, chooses to work with a system of power.

The practice of self-knowledge is both an epistomological and moral undertaking. The "psy discourse" provides a confessional space, and thus subjectifying, technique, where the disclosure of intimate personal details are presented for expert judgement and normative evaluation. Foucault (1986) claims that the state manages the individual by this process of subjectivisation, providing the individual an ethical life in which he monitors, tests and improves the self. The discourse of psychoanalysis is thus a "political technology of the self" where the chosen goal of emancipating the self is what makes the individual manageable and disciplined. Rather than imposing itself between self and society, the self is made to work within a system of power.

The exponents of modernist and postmodernist theory will point us to the dissolution of much more than the medieval monasteries, disconcerting as that was in its time. Instability has replaced stability, transformations are continuous and revolutionary, the transitory has proliferated and proliferates. The contradictions and multiplicities of our current modernity present unprecedented challenges for an overcome the dependable. Whilst post-modernism embraces the excitement of plurality and perpetual motion, expressed in the fleeting image, modernism is more concerned by the abyss that might be revealed alongside the power that individuals or groups might grasp. The enormous technological movements and high speed changes of our times present an ambivalence—where the thrill meets the threat. With an Oedipal echo, we are confronting the place "where three roads meet" (Vickers, 2007) attempting to pursue our exuberant desires whilst dangerously rattling the cage of our limits.

Out of this landscape, the rise of the individual appears unstoppable. For all the freedom that is gained, psychoanalysis would argue that the psyche must be allowed to grow, but with some measure of clipped wings. If we are not able to reflect on and negotiate the losses and limits for ourselves and others we are doomed to dissipation. Our helplessness and dependency also require recognition. Psychoanalytic thinking has something to contribute to what is often alluded to as our narcissistic culture. Contemporary Western culture with its engine room of capitalist consumerism provides a risky place for the ego. Superficiality—and increasingly the experience in which the screen, in all its varieties, dominates as the mirror—provide a depth-less external world which is to be taken in as the "I". Frosh (1991, p. 68) reminds us the hollow dangers beneath the surface stating "the creeping narcissism of our time may sometimes be fun, as self-aggrandisement sometimes is, but ... the end point of narcissism is not the triumph of the self, but its decay". Frosh (1991) argues that our current narcissism is a place where disturbance and normality begin to merge, indicating that the organisation of society, as an external referrant is hugely important in bringing this about. Twelve years earlier, Lasch (1979, p. 23) made similar warnings about the growth of the narcissist: "Fiercely competitive in his demand for approval and acclaim, he distrusts competition because he associates it unconsciously with an unbridled urge to destroy."

With such a responsibility—as not the only, but one very prevalent discourse—psychotherapy would be wise to emphasise its uncomfortable and demanding ethic, of being responsible for ourselves, including our unconscious actions and thoughts. Equally, it might be more explicit about the rigours of well-conducted therapy, where attendance, timing, and payment are demanded to facilitate the process—let alone the potentially disconcerting and anxiety-provoking content of a relationship that requires a re-evaluation of habits and thoughts held dear, however self-destructive. "At its best psychoanalysis is curious and provocative, analysing what is going on without falling into the trap of making simplistic prescriptions for change ... . something serious, slow, thoughtful, uncertain and complicated" (Frosh, 2012, p. 14).

## Current critiques

Psychoanalytic theory maintains an ethical position about the subject taking responsibility for its desires and actions, however painful that process might need to be, where external environmental realities have required much separation. Some aspects of the "therapy culture" that has sprung out of the twentieth-century explorations of the self or subjective experience run the risk of supporting the ego and its denial of reality. This can be heard in Pilgrim's claim of solipsism:

> The problem for psychotherapy is that its tradition of privacy and its preoccupation with the quicksilver of the inner life has exposed it to the criticism on the first count, about external referrants, that it is arcane, solipsistic and unaccountable. On the second count ... it is vulnerable to the criticism that explanations are only conceded at an individual social level. (Pilgrim, 1997, p. 23)

This therapy culture has arguably grown like moss over the true lawn and led to credible "anti-therapy" criticism. Psychotherapies that promote reflective thinking and personal responsibility are a far cry from what Furedi (2004, p. 203) describes as therapy which seeks to "exercise control not through a system of punishment, but through cultivating a sense of vulnerability, powerlessness and dependence. Worst still, contemporary culture fosters a climate where people really do feel ill, insecure and emotionally damaged." It is hard to disagree with his claim that "The call for self-acceptance represents a roundabout way of avoiding change. This conservative orientation towards the future is clearly reflected in the role of therapy itself" (Furedi, 2004, p. 204).

It is arguable that not only the practice, but also the ethics of certain perceived therapies, may indeed to turn the self on itself, seeking for support and inclusion—and at worst are a collusion with the darker potential of narcissism. As practitioners, how are we to challenge demands to promote and shore up the demands of an "I" when it resists the presence, cost, and demand of the "Other"? And how did we come to this? Cultural analysts such as Reiff and Furedi explain the rise of the therapeutic culture as the offside of modernity. Furedi (2004) laments an erosion of solidarity and communal norms and traditional authorities leading to private, individualised personal experience. The individual has become disenfranchised from external authority, leading to anxieties about how to conduct life—and tendencies to exert authority where external forces have declined.

Reiff's *The Triumph of the Therapeutic* (2006) was futuristic about the role psychotherapeutic development would play in the modern world. Reiff is deeply ambivalent about Freud's contribution to society in the creation of what he termed "psychological man", seeing the analytic endeavour as not much more than a remould of the ancient despair–hope dualism, now framed as unconscious–conscious, internal–external. His thorough critique is often pertinent, however. Reiff (2006, p. 220) states: "If yesterday's analytic is to become part of tomorrow's super-ego, it must take on an institutional form, defend itself as not only true but also as good and dig into the personality as a demand system". This call for psychotherapists and analysts to present and defend their own ethic, is echoed in Frosh's quote at the beginning, that it is not us who are getting on with it. The majority of critique on psychoanalysis is being conducted by historians, sociologists, anthropologists, and psychologists—whilst the analytic/psychotherapy profession itself remains occupied with inter-disciplinary debate around schools of thought and role definition, thus missing the social implications that the therapeutic endeavour is having elsewhere.

The sociologist Eva Illouz (2008, p. 1) introduces her study, *Saving the Modern Soul*, with an observation that:

> the therapeutic persuasion is quintessentially modern and that it is modern in what is most disquieting about modernity: bureaucratisation, narcissism, the construction of the false self, the control of modern lives by the state, the collapse of cultural and moral hierarchies, the intense privatisation of life cause by capitalist social organization, the emptiness of the modern self from communal relationships, large-scale surveillance, the expansion of state power and state legitimization, the "risk society" and the cultivation of the self's vulnerability.

Illouz's critique acknowledges the suspicions that have often attended psychoanalysis, the most current contension being that a broad and disseminated therapeutic discourse revolves around an empowering individualism which erodes social relations and commitment to social institutions.

But Illouz is more interested in the how and why of the therapeutic triumph, rather than the fact of its acknowledged success. She proposes that therapy provided a new language of the self which reformulated identity symbols and acknowledges that the therapeutic endeavour, as a cultural framework, achieved considerable influence on concepts of selfhood. Part of the strength of that influence has come about through the presentation of therapeutic knowledge, as disseminated through theories and texts by experts, through all media outlets and ultimately through social institutions, including the workplace and the family, organising social relations in these spheres. Illouz (2008, p. 8) oberserves that:

> the therapeutic discourse offers an entirely new cultural matrix— made of metaphors, binary oppositions, narrative schemas, explanatory frameworks—that throughout the twentieth century has increasingly shaped our understandings of the self and of others.

However, Illouz also goes on to claim that "psychoanalysis" has been one of the "most successful ideas" of our current culture, for fitting in with social structural experiences, such as economic transformation, immigrations, and status anxiety, for providing guidance in conflict-ridden areas such as sexuality, love, and work, and for being institutionalised and part of social networks. Freud might have been delighted by such a conclusion and verifiable parameters in nineteeth-century Vienna and pressed the "like" button—though his own version of achieving this was largely conducted in energising conversations with well-skirted or -jacketed peoples around a seemingly endless number of central European lakes.

Despite this robust and singular claim, Illouz defends her use of the continual generic term "therapeutic" for most of her propositions, arguing that the distinctions between formal and informal knowledge (within which she acknowledges the differences between "painstaking (and costly) therapeutic consultation" and quick-fix self-help literature) must be held lightly aloft when considering the social conditions for their production, the cultural continuities which they suggest, and the own "blurring" which the whole lot of us therapeutic workers must own up to.

## The current cave

With such an ethical potential and actual responsibility, psychotherapy might well ask itself how to pursue into the twenty-first century. Psychotherapists conduct their work with people who have difficulty in living—IN private, IN total confidence, IN discreet settings without signs or advertising, via the means of examining INterior experience to make sense of exterior life. In our current culture of ON-ness—ON line, ON radio, ON Facebook, ON television, ON Twitter, ON billboards—psychotherapy occupies a shadowy place, quite possibly a shadow of an externally fixated ON self-promoting world. Allow for psychotherapy here to be defined as an intervention at the point of suffering, and how we perpetuate suffering—an INquiry into how this came to be and the way through it, conducted withIN a carefully constructed therapeutic relationship. Our own preoccupation with the interiority of our clients and our own internal processing of that work does not lend us to being a vocal, out-there group. We are on the whole poor at publicity and self-promotion, or even at explaining what we do or how we do it. This is at least some explanation, since psychotherapy, as a dynamic, unique to each client process, negotiating unconscious processes endeavour, leaves us with our own core of mystery—which we are doomed (possibly quite rightly) never to feel confident in having mastered.

Critics of psychotherapy are social commentators who point to the ways in which the therapeutic endeavour is not much more than another example of the seductive consumption which pervades society—a self-absorption which has replaced cultural ideals and citizenship. Psychotherapy has failed to demonstrate the links of the private with the public. As shown earlier, Rose (1999) sees the self in therapy as working within a system of power, where the political rationales of free choice result in an injunction to realise one's motives, decisions, and aspirations—to be fulfilled and autonomous. Also, there is indeed Illouz's (2008) new language of the self, whose semantics are widely used to address and examine our emotions, desires, and memories.

Responding to the critique of Reiff and others, we can point out that psychotherapy itself is not solipsistic, but many of its tenets are lost or hidden within a solipsistic culture. Psychotherapy has the potential to, but often failed, to link the private with the public and to that end has allowed itself to become "of its time", rather than anti-doctrine envisioned by Freud. With enthusiasm, Illouz (2008, p. 6) states:

> "Therapy under many forms has been diffused worldwide on a scale that is comparable (and perhaps even superior) to that of American popular culture". Then she hails it as "one of the centers of that amorphous and vague entity known as Western civilization". (p. 6)

There is no doubt that this new language of the self is all-present, but we are so taken up with Pilgrim's "quicksilver of the inner life", that few significant contributions from psychotherapy back into the arena of our culture have been forthcoming.

Frosh (1991) argues that the values of time, uncertainty, and rigorous thinking found in psychoanalytic thought are often unpalatable in a society that favours fast solutions and make it prone to criticisms of being arcane—and acknowledges that its original theories around sexuality and gender have required reworking. However, he is passionate, not only about the influence of analytic theory on all sorts of psychotherapy and counselling, but the role that it is contributing towards social and cultural theory. Indeed, the notions of the unconscious, projection, repression, and so forth are not only used widely to interpret art, literature, and wider social phenomena, but furthermore to enable us to have a language through which to consider the tension between the individual and society. He points out that Freud himself, in his correspondence with Albert Einstein (Freud, 1933b), was called upon to be a social commentator in his time and that he acknowledged the potential of psychoanalysis outside the clinic. However, it is largely social scientists, rather than therapists or analysts, who are taking these thoughts forward in the academic, or wider arena.

## The current knowledge

Psychotherapy possesses its own well-documented symbols and concepts. We are, perhaps, uncomfortable with the knowledge of knowing so. Klein's (1930) concept of the epistemological drive—one in which the search of knowledge drives the subject, holds a paradoxical position within our work. At one level, it is ALL about "knowing" what hasn't been known and symbolised—and at another we seem to deny what is found. It is arguable that we perhaps work with more fixed determinants that we accept: being able to articulate and communicate these is clearly vital to the profession's survival.

Mizen, both a psychologist and a psychoanalyst, points out that although analytic work is a process of discovery (as it was for Freud) with the analyst being "descriptive", something inevitably occurs over time. Mizen (2013, p. 61) observes that "experimental, exploratory and descriptive activity throws up phenomena which have consistency". They are, to a degree, predictable, however much their meaning or significance is in doubt, Mizen notes.

And we know quite a lot. We know that trauma, un-mourned and worked through, incapacitates lives, damaging peace and important relationships. We know that stillbirths and infant deaths are "known" but their implications not made known lead to families struggling with surviving children's psychopathology. We know that present but absent parenthood leads to all sorts. We know that there is an unconscious at play in all things and defences to all that we would rather not know or allow to habituate in our lives. We know that the repetition compulsion (Freud, 1920g) is powerful beyond belief. We know that deprivation—moral, psychological, emotional, and environmental—leads to a marred life, or even a criminal life. We also know that being able to reflect on any of the above releases a freedom to live, not as passive consequences of these things, but despite them. We also know, that in an economically driven and socially constructed world, that those able to live will be able to contribute to stable relationships, family units and able to work. We know that a certain type of talking and listening, in a certain type of relationship can make a difference. We know that suffering does not have to be perpetuated, however undermining or pernicious its influence on our lives.

With such a powerful discourse at our disposal, we might as professionals ask, why we have allowed ourselves been socially and politically muffled, if not worse. Might this be because we also know that establishing person-hood is precarious and that our environment is increasingly in tandem with that fragility? Furthermore, it would appear that within our own profession we have managed to confound ourselves in our own internal briar of theoretical dispute, exemplified since the post-war discourses and onwards to the current contentions around training, frequency, ethics and theory. Mizen (2013, p. 60) points to the current conditions between practitioners where he feels that there is a collusion to deny differences leading to "too little attention to what is distinctive and failing to clarify, refine and develop the work that we do, what we think that we are doing, and how we go about doing it".

Psychotherapy itself was an "anti-doctrine" (Reiff, 2006) against the demands of a culture that could no longer convince. We have perhaps overlooked the moment when "the final demand of privacy collapsed ... and the right to publicity tore therapy out of the hands of Freud and threw it to the swine of the perpetual group grope" (Poulos, 2007, p. 8). In Britain, having recently rallied ourselves around the intrusions by the National Institute for Clinical Excellence (NICE), we have retreated into our own politics around INternal organisations and what they defend against each other. Here, we might remind ourselves of Freud's (1920) surprise, that that death instinct was not directed against the external world, but very disconcertingly upon the self.

Furedi, despite his scathing stance towards therapy, concedes that "although individual therapists sometimes make extravagant claims about the effectiveness of their product, therapeutic culture is distinctly modest about the claims it makes" (2004, p. 104). He observes that this stands in contrast to the way that therapy was promoted in the past and notes the move from "cure" to an "instrument of survival". Whilst noting the disparagement here, if psychotherapy is just that, then it possesses something vitally important—and most clinicians will be aware of life-saving work in their practices.

Frosh's (2012) summary of the contemporary meaning and value that psychoanalytic theory presents is refreshing and workable. He points to how the concepts of the unconscious, defences, transference, and so forth enable us to comprehend our place in the world. Psychotherapy breaks down the opposition between the individual and the social—central to social sciences—and shows how the individual enters social order. Psychotherapy also has well developed concepts capable of reflecting on the phenomena of fantasies, social violence, sexism, racism, and war. Frosh's *Brief Introduction to Psychoanalysis* (2012) is a timely summary of what is worth keeping from the history of psychoanalysis. Somewhat forgotten is the richness of psychoanalysis' origins in post-Kantian, neo-Romantic European culture. Brought about through enquiry and research into the psyche, in a liberal artistic culture developing in Paris, Vienna, Zurich, Prague, and Berlin before the Second World War, psychoanalysis has survived much criticism and pruning. Its legacy for reflecting on psychological life a hundred years later needs not only to be recognised and protected, but defined with relevance to survive into the future.

## The current vocation

This leads me to the question of whether it is possible for the psychotherapy profession to muster its own passion and focus, or indeed whether it might consider it a responsibility to do so. We have our own convictions about what we do, a belief that sound, structured work enables lives to be lived better, with greater fulfilment and less distress for our clients and usually others in their lives. We know that somewhere in our theories we have reliable clues to the nature of human experience and how to better that. But on the whole we remain silent, however. Public-sector psychotherapy is becoming increasingly medicalised. Scientism demands that we explain and justify our outcomes through methodology and research.

Whilst a handful of therapists have written accessible texts around psychoanalytic concepts or their clinical work, there are few psychotherapists, so far, who are drawn to a sort of writing that would be neither a self-help book nor an academic paper. And there are questions to be asked about to whom we are communicating—whether to educate a public we want to engage in the psychotherapeutic process or thought, or a government policy we would like to influence. In terms of what we are saying, might it be possible to recapture passion for the analytic as an ethic, with a moral capacity to call forth a meaningful and self-reflective life? In contrast with a medical model for psychological conditions that separates the illness and the patient, analysis has always offered a relational process, through the transference relationship. Psychotherapy does not settle for the removal of symptoms or correcting behaviours, but believes that a psycho-dynamic change is possible.

Can we find a way of communicating in this world of communication clatter? There needs to be an embrace of a language of relevance and a robustness previously avoided, around the concrete enquiries—does it work, should I want it, should I include it in my organisation or setting? We need to be accountable, not in ways dictated to us by governments, but as advocates of our own profession. If we can avoid theoretical terms and find a working vernacular in our client work, there seems to be no good reason why we cannot reach the general public. We live in an open, global market of screaming vendors, and we would have to join in with similar. We would have to embrace a politically unified voice, using the mediums of the age—advertising, visual communications, and media tools, most of which feel like an anathema to our private, interior leanings.

The nature of our practice, conducted from most theoretical positions, has contributed to this situation. Its possible that our own theories of the transference, the "blank screen", and hiding behind couches have resulted in our own invisibility. It is possible to propose that the uncompromisable ethic of confidentiality regarding what takes place with our clients has resulted in a distorted sense for the need to be confidential about ourselves, our experiences as therapists, and our findings from our clinical work. It is easy to foresee that without setting out our position in twenty-first-century society, psychotherapy will end up without one. We will remain undefined and obscure, shrouded in invisibility that mirrors the shame of "being in therapy" that some of our clients carry.

Whilst the main tenets of psychotherapy are everywhere in modern psy-culture, we are difficult to define and perceive as a distinct profession or theoretical foundation, or even as an ideology. "Personal life cannot survive unless it is embodied in actual practices, institutions and unless it is related to broader understanding of society and history"

(Zaretsky, 2005, p. 342). These institutions may need revising if they are to encapsulate, with optimism, the legacy of psychoanalysis and hand the baton on to future generations.

Unless psychotherapy learns to position itself, a society that does not understand us, even at the level of everyday knowledge, will not be able to benefit from what psychoanalysis can offer and what our culture urgently needs. Psychotherapeutic understanding and clinical practice have the potential to prevent relationship breakdowns and economic instability, can make significant contributions to mental and physical health issues, can help to make sense of suffering, and enable families to stay together. But we need to generate culturally viable ways of putting this forth.

## References

Breuer, J., & Freud, S. (1893). *Studies on Hysteria. SE. 2*: 1–309. London: Hogarth.

Foucault, M. (1979). *Discipline and Punish: The Birth of the Prison*. New York: Vintage.

Freud, S. (1920g). *Beyond the Pleasure Principle. SE. 18*: 1–64. London: Hogarth.

Freud, S. (1933b). Why War? Correspondence with Albert Einstein. http://www.scrbd.com/doc/8267730 (accessed on 17 December 2013).

Frosh, S. (1991). *Identity Crisis: Modernity Psychoanalysis and the Self*. New York: Palgrave Macmillan.

Frosh, S. (2012). *A Brief Introduction to Psychoanalytic Theory*. Basingstoke: Palgrave Macmillan.

Furedi, F. (2004). *Therapy Culture*. London: Routledge.

Illouz, E. (2008). *Saving the Modern Soul*. Oakland, CA: University of California Press.

Klein, M. (1930). The importance of symbol formation in the development of the ego. In: *The Writings of Melanie Klein, Vol. 1* (pp. 219–232). London: Hogarth, 1975.

Lasch, C. (1979). *The Culture of Narcissism*. London: Abacus.

Lasch, C. (1991). *The True and Only Heavens: Progress and its Critics*. New York: Norton.

Mizen, R. (2013). On session frequency and analytic method. *British Journal of Psychotherapy, 29*: 57–74.

Pilgrim, D. (1997). *Psychotherapy and Society*. London: Sage.

Poulos, J. (2007). Philip Reiff, modern prophet. *The University Bookman, 45(2)*: 4–9.

Reiff, P. (2006). *The Triumph of the Therapeutic*. Delaware: ISI Books.
Rose, N. (1999). *Governing the Soul*. London: Free Association Books.
Sass, L. A. (1992). *Madness and Modernism*. Cambridge, MA: Harvard University Press.
Vickers, S. (2007). *Where Three Roads Meet*. Edinburgh: Canongate.
Zaretsky, E. (2005). *Secrets of the Soul*. New York: Vintage.

CHAPTER FIVE

# Psychotherapy, relationality, and the Long Revolution

*Mary MacCallum Sullivan and Harriett Goldenberg*

T his chapter will explore whether and how psychotherapy may
have something to offer beyond the consulting room; whether
this living craft can participate in "the great process of change",
the developmental curve of what is proposed as an historical process
of transformation, a transition from an age of scientific reductionism
to an understanding of the importance of complexity and emergence,
named by cultural critic Raymond Williams as "the Long Revolution"
(Williams, 1961, 2011). The scale of the whole process thus described by
Williams, is, he points out, too large and too "long" to know or even
imagine, but rests, first, on a methodology of self-reflectivity; second,
on an emphasis on relationships and inter-relationship; and third, on
human lived experience. Williams sees revolution, in this sense, as "the
inevitable working through of a deep and tragic disorder", to which we
can respond in different ways. He goes on to argue that "the absolute
test by which revolution can be distinguished, is the change in the form
of activity of a society, in its deepest structure of relationship and feeling" (Williams, 1961, 2011, p. x).

This chapter argues that the practice of relational psychotherapy has
a part to play in such a Long Revolution.

## The age of austerity and the loss of shared meaning

"[T]he capitalist social order has ... done its main job of implant-ing a deep assent to capitalism even in a period of its most evident economic failures" (Williams, 1983, p. 254). This statement still holds good at the time of writing: amidst all the austerities of the post "banking bubble" years, no clear and cogent alternative to capital-ism, globalisation, and the hegemony of free markets has yet been articulated.

The deep, impersonal logic of the market (Barnett, 2011) treats eve-rything, both people and the resources of the planet, as raw material. There is no room in this Hobbesian perspective for human subjectiv-ity; the economic bottom line dictates all, the tail wags the dog. In the face of the necessity to reduce national deficits, after public bail-out of "too large to fail" private banks, governments struggle to remember their duty of care to their citizens ("we are all in this together"), to demonstrate "fairness" in the distribution of meagre resources. Those citizens who are "unproductive" are left behind to fend for themselves, as public subsidies for "good works" disappear into the maw of public debt, which nevertheless stubbornly refuses to diminish, because economic growth is elusive. It is hard to see where demand can be stimulated, how an impoverished and insecure populace can dare to consume more, in the context of a high probability of further economic gloom.

There is a tendency in public and political discourse to speak and think within a modernist, instrumental template that sees persons as individuals (single persons, divided out from the others), making "rational" choices. This perspective is rooted in a Cartesian, Western, Enlightenment world-view, that privileges thinking, for example, over feeling, quantitative over qualitative measure, that relies on a Newtonian scientific understanding of "the world", indeed, that ele-vates such a science to the status of religion.

The American novelist Marilynne Robinson articulated a power-ful critique of the clinging to rationality as an overarching value in her Terry Lectures, delivered at Yale University in 2009: "the mind, as felt experience, has been excluded from important fields of modern thought" and as a result "our conception of humanity has shrunk". To promote such a "closed ontology", she points out, is to deny "the beauty and the strangeness" of the embodied human mind. Subjectivity "is the ancient haunt of piety and reverence and long, long thoughts ..." (Robinson, 2010, p. 35). Robinson recognises that it is subjectivity which gives meaning to the individual herself or, perhaps more importantly, gives a shared meaning that holds both meaning and a sense of belonging. Without awareness and inclusion of subjectivity, Robinson views the modernist perspective of human society as "completely in thrall to the selfish gene" (ibid.).

Yet the contours of an evolutionary paradigm shift are becoming visible, towards "a science of qualities" (Goodwin, 1994), developing awareness of open, complex, self-organising, adaptive systems across the whole of the natural world, including that of human social organisation. Such a shift suggests that the days of the currently dominant "quasi-market" model of social relations may be numbered in favour of an understanding of human societies as "not mere aggregates of selfish and competing individuals but living totalities in which the life of the whole exceeds the sum of the parts; individuals are phenomenologically embodied and embedded in culture and nature which must be seen as inextricably intertwined and co-dependent and co-evolving" (Wheeler, 2006, p. 41). Rather, even, than an "in-dividual", twenty-first-century relational psychotherapy demonstrates that the human being is more a "thing of shreds and patches", a multi-selved being, embodied in animal flesh, embedded in a network of continually changing relationships of different kinds, and moving and being moved in a responsive relationship to such a context. Certain continuities obtain, but often what makes me "me" can be inchoate and intangible at best.

As we struggle with questions of identity, we have trouble acknowledging our real agency, the way our underlying assumptions shape "the world": recognising that only through us does the world become what it is; such intelligibility and order as we find in the way things are is there because we make it so. Like God, we have made the world what it is out of chaos, and, if we don't remain engaged in this task of creation and repair, continually making and remaking the frame of our existence, the world will be the worse for it. Human society in all its dimensions is in a state of dynamic disequilibrium, which makes us fearful of change, of challenge. As members of the social herd, we look to someone else to take responsibility; we look for someone to blame; we demand compensation or retribution for human fallibility as it affects us. We look for easy, reductionist solutions to the dilemmas of human existence; we collude in the delusion that if we put right this little bit here, that little bit there, we have no need to change our model of the human context, to look more deeply within ourselves, and between ourselves and to act in accordance with what that more complex reality. We rationalise human existence into a simplistic set of variables that occlude the importance to each and every one of us of our unique subjectivity, of the affect, the desire, and the deep currents of experience and trauma that underlie and shape our smallest actions and behaviours. Politicians and other policy-makers are not exempt from such tendencies.

Electorates and their media collude with politicians in their presentation of themselves and their parties as heroes, who can fix problems, provide solutions to society's problems. It's a seductive image, an enticing promise. And we keep believing that somewhere there must be a leader who is visionary, inspiring, brilliant, trustworthy, to whom we can happily entrust our vote and give away our power.

As we see the our social realities become more globalised, more complex, there is an assumption that leadership is more efficiently realised within models of command and control that require those at the bottom of the hierarchy to submit to the greater vision and expertise of those above. Leaders promise to get us out of this mess; we willingly surrender individual autonomy in exchange for security.

## Is there another way?

Alternative prescriptions are thin on the ground, but there are some green shoots of hope.

The BBC's 2009 Reith Lectures, entitled *A New Citizenship*, addressed the prospect of a new politics for the common good, articulating the importance of community. Michael Sandel was the speaker, and he has also meticulously argued against the influential doctrine that the economic approach to "utility maximisation" explains all human behaviour. Sandel is unambiguously clear that markets have a moral impact on the goods that are traded in them: he describes a dual phenomenon: the wealthy are able to purchase their way out of the common life (for example, paying homeless people to hold their place in a queue), and through these kinds of practices, both degrade shared values and spread a process of marketisation and corruption (Lanchester, 2012; Sandel, 2009, 2012).

Simon Critchley describes an atmosphere of political disappointment: "the sense of something lacking or failing …, is acutely tangible at the present time, with the corrosion of established political structures and an unending war on terror where the moods of Western populations are controlled through a politics of fear managed by the constant threat of external attack" (Critchley, 2007, p. 3) and proposes to address this disappointment via "a theory of ethical experience and subjectivity that will lead to an infinitely demanding ethics of commitment and politics of resistance" (ibid.).

Occupy protests and demonstrations have spread from Wall Street to London to Bogota. The underpinning idea of the Occupy movement is not simply protest at the unequal distribution of wealth and influence, looking for representation of the interests of "the 99%", or the "common good":

> We believe that we need to reimagine our economic life in a spirit of hope and realism. We want to see our shared imagination shaped by the task of reducing inequality, ending poverty, ensuring sustainability and promoting mutuality,—a task rooted in our understanding of and commitment to the common good. (Church of Scotland, 2012)

But its methodology, which privileged free discussion and debate throughout the community to develop the articulation of aims from the bottom up, rather than from the top down: to listen to the concerns of the participants, and from out of the conversation, to develop a new, shared, narrative and meaning—a meaning that includes the idea of an economics for "the greater good", "as if people mattered" (Schumacher, 1973)—which will then act as a framework for action. Various projects are being developed that move forward such a vision, and a Bank of England official has praised the protest movement, saying Occupy was right not just "in a moral sense", but also in its analysis of the flaws of the banking sector. This was subsequently demonstrated also by the outcomes of investigations into the conduct of various aspects of the activities of Barclays, Royal Bank of Scotland, and Hong Kong and Shanghai Bank. The challenge faced by Occupy and other such movements is how to grow without becoming instruments of the systems they contest (Grusky et al., 2013).

The "Arab Spring", a wave of civil protest, demonstrations, and uprising that has swept the Arab world since the beginning of 2011, has been underpinned by the effective use of new technologies and social media to organise, communicate, and raise awareness in the face of state attempts at repression, as well as to share techniques of civil resistance including strikes, marches, and rallies. This development has overturned an entrenched perception, rooted in "Orientalism" (Said, 1978), that Arab personality and culture were inimical to the project of democracy.

Wheatley and Frieze (2011) suggest that if we want to be able to encompass a more complex understanding of the processual qualities of how societies operate, we need to abandon our reliance on the illusion of the heroic leader and invite in the leader-as-host. We need leaders who know that in order to understand the full complexity of any issue, all parts of the system need to be invited in to participate and contribute. We, as followers, need to be willing to step up and contribute.

Leaders-as-hosts would have to be frank enough to admit that they don't necessarily know what to do; but that they can invite others to participate in collaboratively developing strategies to address problems, that they can listen to others, demonstrating trust in other people's creativity and commitment.

In all of the developments cited above, new technologies and media are influencing public discourse, reshaping social relationships and acting as a medium for revolutionary association, resistance and action.

Such straws in the wind (and many others can be found … .) may herald change; along with Raymond Williams, we wonder whether these developments demonstrate a gathering confidence in our own energies and capacities (rather than those of our leaders) to propose change in the terms of the public conversation (Judt, 2010) change in the "structures of feeling" that, subtly and intangibly, underpin the inevitabilities of the predominant, TINA (There Is No Alternative) mindset. For Williams, "It is only in a shared belief and insistence that there are practical alternatives that the balance of forces and chances begins to alter", and he continues, "Once the inevitabilities are challenged, we begin gathering our resources for a journey of hope" (Williams, 1983, p. 268).

We maintain that psychotherapy—a new "technology"—has developed a methodology for the development of such a shared belief that alternatives exist. Working in collaboration with our clients and patients is nothing if not a journey of hope. We seek to facilitate change at a "deep" level, and often at an individual level; can we imagine that psychotherapy might participate in a much larger-scaled pattern of change, in that context that we describe as "society"?

Psychotherapy has begun, almost imperceptibly, to change the way that human subjectivity is understood, to change our understanding of what is required to make successful relationships—to make a good job of parenting, for example. Psychotherapy, psychoanalysis, counselling, and related disciplines and activities, are beginning to change the way we think (and feel) about human interaction and relationship and may indeed be revolutionary, if realised and accepted within the field of public and political policy.

## *Psychotherapy*

Psychotherapy arguably suffers (in comparison with, for example, the "science" of psychology) from being a living craft, a set of relational skills which only come to life when utilised in a carefully managed conversation with an Other—person, couple, family, or group. My limited aim in this work is to manage to "be-with" the Other, to be consistently available and attuned to the Other with whom I am engaged, to recognise myself as a part of an open, complex, self-organising, adaptive system. This methodology is supported by my personal and professional qualities as a practitioner, seeking generally to demonstrate a consistently positive stance in relation to each and every client, in a reasonably warm and "human" fashion that seeks actively to minimise the asymmetry of power in the relationship. There is a mounting body of evidence indicating that such an approach seems generally a constructive, reparative process, that can be shown to create the possibility of personal and interpersonal change and development, however the individual, couple, family, or group may define this. Such is the "therapeutic attitude".

This attitude, however, often conflicts with our deep-seated, adaptive tendencies towards self-preservation and self-defence; it is, to a degree, an "unnatural" stance. In the context of psychotherapy, we seek to have developed an improved capacity to notice how easy it is to become defensive; we practise becoming more able to acknowledge and work through our defensiveness in certain ways (normally via our own personal therapy or professional supervision). But we recognise that we are still and always programmed or hard-wired for self-interest, survival, and self-protection, which includes powerful mechanisms for deception and self-deception (Smith, 2004; Trivers, 1985), and we'd be fools to imagine we are any better than anybody else at getting around that. Hopefully we learn, through training and praxis, and through attention to our own personal process, that it is possible to choose to adopt other modes of being, ways of more fully "being-for-the-other", that can be learned and supported.

Doing this work professionally may not initially be seen by outsiders, or even by beginning trainees, as such a big deal, but it takes time, perhaps, for the scale of the challenge to make itself realised: training to become a psychotherapist or counsellor takes the form of a direct, existential, challenge to the individual to come out of the crowd and take upon herself the burden and the responsibility of being-for this other, the client, within these very particular parameters, or boundaries. Throughout training, it takes practice, private and shared reflection, and a continued wrestling with the ethical endeavours of the work and with one's own self-orientated conditioning and defences, to make a competent practitioner. As it challenges our adaptive tendency towards deception and self-deception, the training draws on and develops what has been proposed as a universal human reparative impulse (Judaism's *tikkun olum*, or Christian kingdom theology): seeing something wrong, or lacking, and wanting to do something to facilitate repair of what has been damaged or is lacking for the other.

So how can the therapeutic attitude be translated into the public sphere?

## *I, you, and it*

A foundational skill of psychotherapy is the neglected craft of listening, paying attention to the nature of language, and to our embeddedness in it.

Human communication is multi-levelled: it is used to seek and to give information, to communicate and hide feeling, to give and seek "strokes", to seek personal or professional advancement or attachment, to deceive. We exist in language, are shaped by language; we use language consciously and unconsciously. We also communicate through the body (gesture, posture, gait, body "armour" (Reich, 1942), illness, medical conditions), expression (facial muscles, eyes, hands), silence, action ("acting out"). The quality of "presence" of an individual is more than the sum of these parts; intention, discipline, attention, can be communicated by action (or inaction), behaviour, and by the physical environment we expect or accept, by the way in which we manage ourselves.

When we listen, we are using the language, the style of communication of the speaker as a resource. We observe and make mental notes, absorbing impressions, seeking to notice the trivial, the "unconscious", jokes, body language, missing or denied words, repudiated meanings. The intention to enter a true relation with the other, becoming attuned to her mode of being, her world-view, and the possibility of constructing shared meaning rests on competence in the language of the other, rather than merely the imposition of our own conceptual framework.

An aspect of that competence in listening, is the capacity to set aside my own desire, my preoccupation, my biases and assumptions, to situate myself in a place of un-knowing. I thus set aside, or at least temporarily "bracket", whatever my wished-for outcome of the present activity may be. This encourages me also to set aside my own normal, "social" need to contribute in a "tit-for-tat" conversational style, or to ask questions to feed my need to "understand". It's good to wait, and wait again. It is surprising how often, if I wait, my questions will be answered. The discipline of this initial silence often seems to free me from the need to respond and allows me to relax into listening and observing.

When we attend closely, we notice the speaker's state of mind/body, whether and to what degree is she relaxed or tense. We notice what changes and when; we notice the "shape" of the speaker's discourse. What we also seek to notice and to wonder about is how my presence and mode of being influences and affects the other, because how I am and what I say, or don't say, and how this is understood by the other, are key elements in the context of our meeting. Whatever the purpose of the encounter, it will stand or fall on the personal qualities of the protagonist with the "lead role" or with the responsibility of managing the encounter; it will stand or fall on the basis of the relationship created, on the quality of the relationality, be it for one hour or for much more.

According to Martin Buber (1958), our human response to others, consists in two basic relational attitudes: *I–Thou* or *I–It*. The *I–Thou* relation is constituted as subject-to-subject, while the *I–It* is a relation of subject-to-object. If I am able to maintain a sense of the other as a subject like myself, I relate to the other as a complex human being, and engage in a dialogue of equals involving each other's whole being. If I lapse into the *I–It* relationship, I am liable to perceive the other as consisting of some specific, isolated qualities, and view her as part of a world that consists of things. I may view her as "the client", as "the consumer", as a member of "the public", as a representative of a particular demographic. The *I–Thou* is a relationship of mutuality and reciprocity that embraces the subjectivity and complexity of the Other, while the *I–It* is a relationship of separateness, detachment, objectification, alienation, which denies the richness and uniqueness of the Other. The challenge is to maintain that relational attitude in different social and interpersonal contexts and to be open to what may flow from that.

Such a relational attitude sits awkwardly with a top-down policy development model that sets out to map the probable priorities of different demographic groups and tailors policy and presentation towards "pressing the buttons". The relationship is of political party or governing elite "selling" to a consuming electorate or "public". Examples of reciprocal, or *I–Thou*, relationships between, say, elected representatives and those they represent may be confined to local "surgeries"; the fault-lines in the relational attitude appear with the distinction between representation and policy development or implementation, and the entanglements and seductions of power relations.

But reciprocity can also be between groupings, organisations, levels of organisation: the project of the European Community/Union has precisely been about binding nations together into reciprocal relations, with some functions and powers ceded to the "supersystem" others remaining with the nations, and yet others devolved to constituent regions, with an explicit aim to create a more level playing field and to avoid conflict getting out of hand, as in two world wars. The vision (however imperfectly realised thus far) is of collaboration, reciprocity, and dialogue between nations and, within nations, between the state, community organisations, and citizens.

Another key component of the therapeutic attitude is "being-with".

> Much of what takes place within therapy is precisely this struggle to be-with-an-Other, to "be-together", a struggle for both client and therapist. Each comes with different expectations of the other and themselves, and there is an allocation (implicitly, or explicitly) of different tasks. For instance, my task as therapist may be to attempt

to enter into the world of my client; to acknowledge my client as "Other", while recognising we are both "one of the others". (MacCallum Sullivan & Goldenberg, 2003, p. 50)

The example of the Occupy movement suggests a methodology of hosting meetings or sessions where participants get to speak and be listened to in a spirit of dialogue, where divergent subjectivities participate, opposing views are expressed, differing priorities promoted, but where informed consensus is sought, and compromises hammered out through discussion and in light of available resources. This bottom-up approach is likely to be resisted where proposed action may conflict with existing power structures or overarching policies, and speaks precisely to the need in the UK for a strengthening of local government and a subsidiarity that would require a radical departure from the current centralised model of tightly imposed financial control.

And, finally, it is the idea of relationality itself that constitutes a paradigm shift in psychotherapy, and, hopefully, in other contexts. In psychotherapy, the trend in research evidence is demonstrating that "modality", the technical approach is, initially at least, irrelevant to outcome; qualities of acceptance, relational trustworthiness, provision and maintenance of a "safe", reliable, and consistent environment are more significant. The significance of the relational context has come to the fore through the development of Bowlby's attachment theory and its burgeoning body of research, via observation made possible through the use of film and video in infant research, where baby-and-others are observed in moment-by-moment real time, and via the new technologies available to observe, track, and map responsive activity in the human brain—CAT, PET, and other forms of electronic scanning.

But it is also in the laboratory of the therapeutic session, constructed within clear ethical boundaries, that we see the moment-to-moment reciprocal rhythm and to-and-fro-ness of human interaction. In a close reading of the "text" of the therapeutic material, we see how the one affects and "regulates" the other, how the moving "power" within the interaction flows from the one to the other. The therapist hopes to be responsive to the expression of the client, but even so can be taken aback at how sensitively attuned to her words, or even non-verbal responses and interventions, her client can be.

How well can the professional therapeutic relationship be transposed to other professions and contexts?

A programme, based on initial projects in Dundee, and initiated by the UK Coalition Government in 2011 requires:

> a single dedicated worker to walk in the shoes of these families every day. To look at the family from the inside out, to understand its dynamics as a whole, and to offer practical help and support— but also to be the person to authoritatively challenge that family to change. (Casey, 2012, p. 4)

A worker "got to know" all of the family members and found out about their problems. She spent considerable time with each of the individual children. As relationships were built,

> the family members revealed to her their differing desires, traumas and losses. The interventions of the dedicated worker within the context of "relationship" and in response to awareness of these concerns were instrumental in supporting the families to change. (Casey, 2012, p. 16)

> If practitioners can overcome families' resistance and start to build such relationships, families are much more likely to accept the support being offered and respond to the strong challenge to try to change their lives. (ibid., p. 17)

> Family intervention workers are dedicated to the families and provide an antidote to the fragmented activity from many different agencies that usually surrounds a troubled family. They "grip" the family, their problems and the surrounding agencies and are seen to be standing alongside the families, their difficulties and the process being put in place, which can lead to new approaches to dealing with long standing problems. (ibid., p. 18)

The outcomes from these interventions, requiring concentrated attention, "being-with", and therapeutic "holding" ("grip"), within clearly delineated boundaries of shared responsibility, have been striking.

### And from the "how" comes learning

From out of the "techniques" and attitudes, developed through the working-through that is psychotherapeutic praxis, learning, or "wisdom", has come. We have learned that "bad behaviour" is usually understandable as a response to trauma or loss. The experience of trauma, in many different forms, some of which may be invisible to the naked eye, is something that is common to us all. We have learned that each and every human being has their own experience of relational trauma, has sought to overcome, has adopted strategies towards psychic survival, towards a productive relational life, some more successful than others. We have learned that who we are is constructed out of our subjective relational experience, which in recessive turn is shaped by our relational history.

We have learned of the trauma inflicted by loss in its many forms, whether by our experience of abandonment, or in some of the more obvious and visible ways that children suffer, from stereotyping, marginalisation, neglect, cruelty, and abuse. We have learned that resilience grows out of our experience of being loved and cared for, of being "recognised", and of being able to transmute that into a sense of agency, relative autonomy, and personal capability. We have learned about how paramount for the adult is the "good-enough" experience of a responsive and attuned human environment in the first years of life.

We have learned about the damaging effect of a corrosive lack of respect in our culture for the experience of childhood (Miller, 1987) and particularly towards boys, and that boys suffer from the still-predominant "taboo on tenderness" (Suttie, 1988) that continues to hold sway in the wider social context.

We have learned that relationship is all: "there is no such thing as an individual". I am always in relationship with myself, with a partner, with parents, with children, with wider family, with friends, with colleagues, or just with passers-by; with the organisations within which I work, to which I am affiliated, or on which I depend. I inhabit all of these relationships; they determine my "structures of feeling"; they offer me identity, belonging, a meaning to my life. This learning gives the lie to the splendid isolation and abstraction of the Cartesian *Homo sapiens*, the thinking being—a fantasy, a defensive aspiration, but centrepiece of economists and political advisors.

## From relational psychotherapy to the common good

Margaret Thatcher is reputed to have declared, "There is no such thing as 'society'". To the contrary, we have discovered, through the ecological sciences, through complexity theory, through space travel, through the praxis of relational psychotherapy, that we are all part of each other, that we are all more part of each other than we have ever been, arguably, from one extreme of this small blue planet to the other: "The concept 'individual' refers to interdependent people in the singular, and the concept 'society' is interdependent people in the plural" (Elias, 1978, p. 124).

My addiction to driving contributes to the sinking of small pacific nation states beneath the waves of that great ocean; the inequalities in wealth, resources and opportunity within and between nations is, in and of itself, experienced as violence, hurting both those with and those without: the rich more and more withdraw behind walls and gates, fostering debilitating fantasies of fear of invasion, as the poor, displaced from connection to place and rootedness in the earth, huddle in camps, subsisting or slowly starving.

That there is no such thing as society allows and facilitates division, lack of social mobility, and inequality. The lives of individual "citizens" (subjects?) are seen, for practical purposes, through the prism of the needs of the established order as material for, or obstacle to, "growth", as the assumed overarching purpose of "society" (Williams, 1961, 2011).

Practitioners of relational psychotherapy are, in some ways, the same as the cloistered religious whose aim is to support the world through their prayers and religious practice (Kowalska, 2005); privacy and confidentiality is core to our work; we are turned away from the outside world, finding our own personal meaning in the work, as well as proposing to be helpful to clients and patients engaged in the same quest. Yet we are in denial of our role in the external context of our work, with which, of course, we, and our clients, are intimately intertwined. It is sometimes difficult to reconcile ways of speaking out, seeking influence, with our need, or preference, for professional discretion and anonymity.

Psychotherapy, counselling, and psychoanalysis are also marginalised in terms of professional status, because of the discipline's ambiguous relationship to the prevalent requirements for "evidence-based" practice. Yet, as "a subjectively impassioned pursuit of an empirically based science" (Wheeler, 2006, p. 50), psychotherapy sits alongside many emerging branches of the new "science of qualities" which recognises the complexity of the "human in its environment".

So, if "society" is more neutrally defined as a flexible human organisation, the cumulation of our social relationships, we can determine radically to revise our conception of ourselves in society to take account of our "evidence-based" understanding of what is required better to support human creativity and well-being.

Williams (1961, 2011) offers a powerful analysis of the consequences of our despair at finding ourselves outnumbered and outgunned by the current "givens" of our social context, by a sense of its essential impersonality, the narrow concentrations of actual power; "no people live here, only classes, consumers and conventions" (Williams, 2011, p. 138). But we have felt our sphere of possible reaction to be limited to withdrawal into individualism, such that I and my family, friends, (and clients) are "real people", the "others" can be confined to the *I–It* category as "the public". Such "romantic individualism and authoritarian and abstract social thinking, have again and again, in modern societies, tended eventually to interlock. Power, in such cases, is ultimately rationalized by despair" (ibid.).

Williams goes on to argue, however, that:

> changes in primary relationships, particularly between parents and children, will have observable social effects, and to argue that changes of this kind—the growth of love and the capacity for loving—are fundamental in the development of a society … . much of our deepest humanity is learned in these relationships, but there is also a very deep crisis at the point of transfer of responses and values learned in this close world to the responses and values conventionalized in a working social system. (2011, pp. 147–148)

Through the work in the consulting-room, by all means, but also by coming together with others and acting outwith this private space, creating new structures and ethical rules. The International Co-operative Alliance (2012) sets out its values and principles thus: values of self-help, self-responsibility, democracy, equality, equity and solidarity. In the tradition of their founders, co-operative members believe in the ethical values of honesty, openness, social responsibility and caring for others. We contribute to the transformation and renewal of our social context. We stand up for the validity and usefulness for the public sphere of the "impassioned pursuit of our empirical science"; we insist on the importance for social and political life of complexity and subjectivity, of relationality and interconnectedness.

## References

Barnett, A. (2011). Foreword, to R. Williams, *The Long Revolution*. Cardigan, Ceredigion: Parthian Books.

Buber, M. (1958). *I and Thou* (Trans. R. G. Smith). Edinburgh: T. & T. Clark. (Reprinted from M. Buber, *Ich und Du*, Leipzig, 1923).

Casey, L. (2012). Working with troubled families: a guide to the evidence and good practice. https://www.gov.uk/government/uploads/system/uploads/attachment_data/file/66113/121214_Working_with_troubled_families_FINAL_v2.pdf. (accessed on 15 December 2012).

Church of Scotland (2012). *A Right Relationship with Money*. Special Commission on the Purposes of Economic Activity.

Cooperative Alliance (2012). Values and principles. http://www.co-operative.coop/corporate/aboutus/The-Co-operative-Group-Values-and-Principles/ (acceessed on 20 April 2014).

Critchley, S. (2007). *Infinitely Demanding: Ethics of Commitment, Politics of Resistance*. London: Verso Books.

Elias, N. (1978). *The Civilising Process: The History of Manners*. Cambridge: Cambridge University Press.

Goldenberg, H., & Isaacson, Z. (1996). Between persons: the narrow ridge where I and Thou meet. *Journal of the Society of Existential Analysis, 7*: 118–130.

Goodwin, B. (1997). *How the Leopard Changed Its Spots: The Evolution of Complexity*. London: Orion Books.

Grusky, D. B., McAdam, D., Reich, R., & Satz, D. (Eds.) (2013). *Occupy the Future*. Cambridge, MA: Boston Review.

Judt, T. (2010). *Ill Fares the Land*. London: Penguin.

Kowalska, H. F. (2005). *Divine Mercy in My Soul: The Diary of St. Faustina*. Stockbridge, MA: Marian Press.

Lanchester, J. (2012). *What Money Can't Buy*. Review by Michael Sandel. *The Guardian*, 17 May.

MacCallum Sullivan, M., & Goldenberg, H. (2003). *Cradling the Chrysalis: Teaching/Learning Psychotherapy*. London: Continuum Books.

Miller, A. (1987). *The Drama of Being a Child: The Search for the True Self*. London: Virago.

Reich, W. (1980). *Character Analysis* (Trans. V. Carfagno). New York: Farrar, Straus & Giroux.

Robinson, M. (2010). *Absence of Mind: The Dispelling of Inwardness from the Modern Myth of the Self* (Terry Lectures). Newhaven, CT: Yale University Press.

Said, E. (1978). *Orientalism*. New York: Vintage Books.

Sandel, M. J. (2009). *Justice: What's the Right Thing To Do?* London: Allen Lane.

Sandel, M. J. (2012). *What Money Can't Buy: The Moral Limits of Markets*. London: Allen Lane.

Schumacher, E. F. (1973). *Small Is Beautiful: A Study of Economics as if People Mattered*. London: Sphere/Abacus.

Scottish Community Alliance: http://www.localpeopleleading.co.uk/about/who-we-are/ (Accessed on 20 April 2014).

Smith, D. L. (2004). *Why We Lie: The Evolutionary Roots of Deception and the Unconscious Mind*. New York: St Martin's Press.

Suttie, I. D. (1988). *The Origins of Love and Hate*. London: Free Association Books.

Trivers, R. (1985). *Social Evolution*. California: Cummings/Benjamin.

Wheatley, M., & Frieze, D. (2011). Leadership in the Age of Complexity: from hero to host. *Resurgence, 264*.

Wheeler, W. (2006). *The Whole Creature: Complexity, Biosemiotics and the Evolution of Culture*. London: Lawrence and Wishart.

Williams, R. (1958). *Culture and Society 1780–1950*. New York: Columbia University Press, 1983.

Williams, R. (1961). *The Long Revolution*. Cardigan, Ceredigion: Parthian, 2011.

Williams, R. (1983). *Towards 2000*. London: Hogarth.

# CHAPTER SIX

# Human-based medicine—theory and practice: from modern to postmodern medicine

*Michael Musalek*

T he world of modern medicine is shaped by positivism and revered as a place of reason, a world in which mathematical calculation and "objectivity" are prized above all else. "Evidence-based" has become a buzzword, standing for safety, state of the art and high-quality patient care, while medicine has become a world of sober number games, reduction and fragmentation, demystification and desubjectification. However, much is lost in attaining this so-called objectivity, namely ourselves as human beings. In evidence-based medicine, the suffering human being in all their individuality is sacrificed on the altar of medical research to the manmade construct of disease, which, contrary to its characteristics, is regarded as natural. Surely, this process is only comprehensible as a final act of resistance by a science indoctrinated with positivism and propelled by a drive towards objectivity.

## From eminence-based medicine to evidence-based medicine

The medical approach known as evidence-based medicine has many advantages compared to its predecessor, eminence-based medicine. In the latter, the medical opinion of an expert or group of experts sufficed for a treatment to gain acceptance, with no need for controlled studies.

Every medical intervention is embedded in the prevailing spirit of its time. Today, we are privileged to be living in a period of transition, from modernity based on positivism to postmodernity which rejects ultimate truths and objectivity in the narrow sense (Musalek, 2005). Undoubtedly, the objectification of medical interventions has incalculable advantages. Today's much-praised evidence-based medicine is indebted to the positivism of the modern and its maxims, and accordingly asserts the correctness of its approaches, defined as guidelines that, in deference to ultimate medical truths, must be followed. The basic principle of positivism is the given, the factual, the "positive", and to dismiss as useless all arguments that aim to go beyond this. The only permissible approach for science is to hold to that which is "positive", clear, and perceivable, namely that which can be observed by means of a sensual experience (Blackburn, 1996).

In contrast to positivist philosophy, evidence-based medicine does not view a phenomenon as a "positive fact". Instead, the positive is reduced to one specific manifestation: significant results of cohort studies carried out on the largest possible number of people and calculated using statistical methods, whereby probability is equated with or mistaken for truth. Modern, evidence-based medicine is thus structured on the basis of numbers and founded on the belief that numbers, in particular statistically significant calculations, bestow objectivity and truth. This does not do justice to the meaning of the term "evidence", which is derived from Latin (*evidential*—evident, clarity) and denotes "a general direct certainty, a revelation, insight", the showing-itself of an object or situation, and the resulting intellectual "seeing" or "realisation". Contrasting with "discursive-conceptual insight" (Ulfig, 1999), evidence became the central criterion of truth in the sciences: the greater the evidence, the greater the degree of truth. Evidence thus stands for the greatest consciously experienced insightfulness that leads to certainty. A distinction is made between psychological evidence (feeling of being convinced) and logical evidence bestowing the conviction that the judgement is valid (Schischkoff, 1991).

Such a definition makes clear the subjective character of evidence: it is we who impute evidence to a phenomenon. Yet, these are not well-considered, analytically distant judgements, but a ... direct insight that lays a particular claim to truth. Unlike a truth that is corroborated by proof, evidence is not mediated. It is intuitive, and not discursive. For a long time, the axioms of Euclidean geometry served as the models for evidence (Brockhaus, 2004). Husserl (1939) postulates that the mode of apprehension of evidence is human perception. In the showing-itself of a situation, the evidence is recognised by the apprehending consciousness. It is the immediate evidence of the showing-itself of a situation in itself.

Evidence-based medicine grounded in positivism has a completely different approach. The promoters of evidence-based medicine want nothing to do with subjective judgements, let alone intuition. The showing-itself of a givenness does not wish to be concretised with general perceptions and the idealisations they engender, but by probability calculations. Evidence-based medicine elevates statistical significance to being the sole criterion of truth. Epidemiological studies, controlled cohort comparisons, and biostatistics become masters of the universe (Feinstein, 1985; Kramer, 1988; Weiss, 1986). This was not always the case. David Sackett and colleagues from the Department of Clinical Epidemiology and Biostatistics at MacMaster University in Canada, one of the birthplaces of contemporary evidence-based medicine, define evidence-based medicine as "the conscientious, explicit and judicious use of the current best evidence in making decisions about the care of individual patients … integrating individual clinical expertise with the best available external clinical evidence from systematic research" (Sackett et al., 1996). Sackett et al. (1985) also spoke out against the naïve "scientism" of fundamentalist representatives of evidence-based medicine, stating that evidence-based medicine must not be allowed to become "cookbook medicine". It should inform but never replace individual clinical expertise (Sackett et al., 1996). They emphasised the need for internal and external evidence: the first denotes the conviction of an expert arising from their experience; the second, knowledge gained from cohort studies.

The confusion surrounding the concept of evidence-based medicine at an international level is even more apparent if one bears in mind that the concept was developed in the English-speaking world. "Evidence" in English stands for proof: not the incontrovertible proof provided by mathematics or the natural sciences but the kind of proof put before a court of law (Kühlein & Forster, 2007). Evidence and counter-evidence form the basis for a conclusive judgement; these are not truths in the narrow sense but pointers to possible truths. Evidence is more or less credible. How far removed this concept of evidence is from that advocated by many evidence-based medicine supporters: namely, medicine based on "objective", "scientifically validated" medical truths is the only "true" medicine.

The chief problem with evidence-based medicine lies less in its essential nature and more in the denial of the inherent problems in a rigid and unimaginative interpretation. Only those familiar with its problematic aspects can make meaningful use of evidence-based medicine.

## Problems of evidence-based medicine

Attention has already been drawn to the central problem: equating or confusing truth and probability. The results of statistical calculations are often celebrated as scientific proof while they are simply indicators of certain factual relationships. In addition, there are methodological problems with cohort studies: for example, duration, outcome criteria, selection of patients, comorbidities, control groups, and exclusion criteria. The limitations of collective case studies mean that results can only be considered representative for patients who will ultimately be treated in exceptional cases.

The greatest problem with evidence-based psychiatry lies in the direct transfer of quality assurance measures from medical research to clinical practice. By nature, research projects are reductionist: they simplify the subject or process to be studied. Separation, reduction, and abstraction are the magic words of positivistic empirical research. By contrast, clinical practice must do justice to the complexity of disease and the interactions between disease processes, treatment, and individual character of those being treated. Human beings cannot be reduced to simple machines. There will never be binding "pilot manuals" for treating sick people.

Medicine based solely on evidence-based data therefore must always fall short. David Sackett is right when he says evidence-based medicine requires a "bottom-up approach", integrating the best external evidence with individual clinical expertise and patient choice (Sackett et al., 1996). As important as the achievements of evidence-based medicine are, it needs to be expanded by a medicine that places the person at the centre of diagnosis and therapy in a truly human-based approach (Musalek, 2005, 2008).

## Human-based medicine and its characteristics

How does human-based medicine differ from traditional evidence-based medicine? As mentioned earlier, a key distinguishing factor is the focus of medical intervention. In contrast to conventional "indication-based medicine", with its manmade construction of disease, in human-based medicine the patient in totality is the focal point of diagnostic and therapeutic interest. In addition, human-based medicine is founded on a different philosophy. While evidence-based medicine is indebted to modern positivism, human-based medicine's foundations are based in the maxims of postmodernism. Third, there are differences in diagnostic approach: evidence-based medicine diagnostics are deficiency-oriented and categorical, while human-based medicine pursues resource-oriented, multidimensional diagnostics. The fourth difference lies in patient management. The monologue of modern medicine (Foucault, 1961) becomes a dialogue. No doctor has a monopoly on ultimate truths; the primary objective is to achieve mutual understanding in contrasting worlds of knowledge, enabling therapists and patients to meet on an equal footing and overcoming *Vergegnung* ("mis-meeting": Buber, 1958). The final key difference between evidence-based medicine and human-based medicine is in treatment. There are differing treatment objectives (symptom-killing versus enabling the patient to live as autonomous and happy a life as possible), diverging therapeutic strategies (deficiency-oriented versus resource-oriented), and different forms of treatment (monotherapeutic prescriptive medicine versus dialogue-modular, multidimensional).

## Human-based medicine: foundations

Human-based medicine is indebted to postmodern maxims. The concept of the postmodern is closely associated with the work of the philosopher Jean-François Lyotard (1979), who exposed the philosophical and scientific systems of the world as human *grandes narratives*. The postmodern becomes a reaction against a naïve belief in progress and the scientific truth of a positivistic modernity and rejects conventional realism and fundamentalism (Audi, 1999; Blackburn, 1996). If modernism can be characterised by confidence in steady (economic, technical, scientific) progress, post-modernism discusses its limits (Heckmann &

Lotter, 2004) and becomes an inhomogeneous cultural criticism of the modern age.

Postmodernism encompasses widely divergent positions that leave plenty of room for irony. For many, it is synonymous with ambiguity, imprecision, lack of clarity, and uncertainty. Even if the postmodern realm is characterised by diversity, even dichotomy, Feyerabend's (1975) slogan "anything goes" demonstrates that very few maxims can be considered typical of postmodern thought (Musalek, 2005):

1. There is no single, ultimate truth that can be derived from nature. Truth always depends on the point of reference, the perspective. Different truths can be simultaneously recognised as accurate for the same situation even if they appear contradictory (relativism concept).
2. Objectivity in the sense of access to knowledge that goes beyond subjectivity is rejected. We can never escape subjectivity. All our truths are based on subjective judgements, intuitions, and conclusions (subjectivism doctrine).
3. All truths, principles, circumstances, conclusions, and study results depend on context. They cannot be evaluated independently of their frameworks (context dependency of all being concept).
4. Word and object do not represent a unit broken in two, as the positivistic theory of language would have us believe. On the contrary, "the meaning of a word is its use" (Wittgenstein, 1958). Moreover, the meaning of a word, a sentence, always relates to its historic and cultural context; a change in context induces a change in the meaning of the word (Rohmann, 2001). Language is thus not a determined, stable medium of thinking, the prerequisite for recognition as an ultimate truth (postmodern philosophy of language, poststructuralism constructs).
5. The observer is always a changing element of the system. Whatever and however we analyse, the given is simultaneously changed through our analysis. Analysis becomes a construction process: research results, even those obtained in high-quality, controlled studies, are determined to a significant extent by our questions and the design of our studies. Of course, this creative process does not happen out of nothing; we can only create our worlds within the framework given to us (by nature). The creative process is an interplay between that which is given and that which is made (constructivism concept).

These postmodern maxims run counter to the striving for ultimate truth by modern research and thus to an evidence-based medicine shaped by positivism. Things we believed in the past are shaken to their foundations. This shift inevitably leads to rejection of the postmodern, despite the fact that postmodern maxims offer enormous opportunities for development. For example, the question of whether pharmacotherapy is a more effective treatment for psychological disorders than psychotherapy might be resolved by a postmodern perspective: both views could be seen as true. If a psychological disorder is regarded as a physical occurrence manifesting itself in psychological phenomena, a physical treatment makes sense. If one regards a psychological disorder as a psychological occurrence, with a reflexive relationship with the individual, psychotherapeutic help offers ways of coping or escaping. The same applies to physical disorders and their psychosomatic or psychological aspects. In clinical practice, it is no longer a question of the correct way of looking at something but of looking at the patient and their illness from as many perspectives as possible to provide the maximum number of effective treatments. Postmodernism thus offers the possibility of a paradigm shift in medicine. It allows us to abandon (too) restrictive, modern, evidence-based medical approaches and to develop diagnostic and treatment structures and methods of patient management that do justice to the diversity of human existence.

## Human-based medicine: diagnostics

Moving away from classical "indication-based" medicine towards human-based medicine requires a fundamental change in diagnostics. Traditional categorial diagnostics will not suffice if the focus is no longer the illness construct but the person suffering from the illness. Today's modern diagnostics focuses exclusively on constructs of illness, on manmade, predefined categories, catalogues of characteristics, and related algorithms. Diagnosis serves to reliably assign individual disease characteristics to categories that correspond to symptoms. These become subject to a process of "de-historicisation" (Musalek, 2005), and, in keeping with positivistic thought, become regarded as natural, given categories that can be used as the starting point for research projects and treatment strategies. In clinical practice, these categories of disease may be compared with drawers, opened by means of a correct access code (specific constellations of symptoms or results) and containing specific treatment recommendations for the respective "disease". What all manmade categorial classifications have in common, whether syndromatological or nosological, is that their nature remains untouched and continues to prevail.

However, categories of disease are neither god-given nor facts given to us by nature; they are simple human fabrications (Musalek, 2005). As Nietzsche (1882) knew, "Nature knows no forms and concepts, hence also no species ... but only an X which remains inaccessible and undefinable for us." Of course, it is always we humans who create concepts, definitions, and categories, and it is we who try to classify the nature that surrounds us. Most categorial diagnostic criteria are not even the empirically sound inventions of an individual but the result of agreements reached by bodies of experts: "historic-democratic constructs".

The creation of ICD (International Classification of Diseases) (WHO, 1993) aimed to optimise the comparability of individual diagnostic categories across different institutions, countries, and continents, with the prime objective of increasing the reliability of the individual diagnoses. This approach failed owing to the fundamental problem inherent in all categorial diagnostics, namely, we do not know "true nature" and its principles of classification and, even if such principles exist, we will never be able to recognise them. That which we call the "true" or "real" order of nature is just a manmade classification of the phenomena that face us (Musalek, 2008). "One thinks that one is tracing the outline of the thing's nature over and over again and one is merely tracing round the frame through which we look at it" (Wittgenstein, 1958, p. 48). Knowledge of nature in the sense of understanding the natural given, the "donatum", continues to be denied us. This does not mean we wish to promote a diagnostic nihilism. However, achieving goal-oriented patient management and making sufficient effective treatment options available requires extending conventional categorial diagnostics to include comprehensive, multidimensional diagnostics with therapeutic relevance (Musalek, 2003).

Multidimensional diagnostics must start from the individual phenomenon, questioning its origins and the pathoplastic effect of the particular constellation of conditions, exploring meaning for the individual of the psychopathological phenomena and mental illness as a whole, focusing not only on the deficiencies that arise from the illness but to a large extent on the person's resources (Musalek, 2008). The central diagnostic question in psychiatry is no longer: which mental illness does the patient have and how can it be made to disappear? The questions are: what is the person suffering from in particular and in general; what are the constellations of circumstances; how can they be brought out of their state of suffering and helped to return to as autonomous and happy a life as possible? First and foremost, individual pathological phenomena must be apprehended in their pathoplasticity. Questions about the occurrence of a specific illness are replaced by questions about the temporal, qualitative and quantitative sequences of individual psychopathological phenomena.

In a second step, the constellation of these individual phenomena are examined. In contrast to static, categorial diagnostics, multidimensional diagnostics does not regard a state of illness as something that enters our world but as a dynamic process beginning from predisposition and factors that trigger disease through a course determined by disease-perpetuating factors. It is essential at all stages to apprehend all physical, mental, and social factors, and their interactions, responsible for the disease processes that underlie the materialisation of the individual phenomenon. These aetiological and pathogenetic factors may change during the course of the illness; as disease-perpetuating factors, they keep the pathological process alive and model it. From this perspective, a single differential diagnosis cannot clarify all the relevant pathogenetic factors and a differential diagnosis that continues for the duration of the treatment is required. Thus a differential diagnosis made on a single occasion as a purportedly finished event becomes a process and is reflected in the term "differential diagnostics process".

The main focuses of this process are disease-perpetuating factors (pathogenic factors responsible for the perpetuation of the disease) and the patient's resources, which must be regarded as the most effective counterweight to the former. All physical, mental, and social factors causing the onset of the pathological process can continue to have an effect during the course of the process and become disease-perpetuating factors. Moreover, pathogenic factors are generated by the pathological process itself. Both the momentum of the disease and the meaning the disease takes on for the patient and their environment are to be emphasised (Musalek, 2003). Each disease has a specific momentum which has a pathogenic effect as the illness continues. This momentum is not limited to the person who is ill; it is intertwined with the patient's environment. With a few exceptions (for example, affective disorders, delusional disorders, or addictive disorders), there is a relative paucity of knowledge about these self-reinforcing processes.

In addition to its momentum, it is the meaning of a disease that can become a disease-perpetuating factor. Every disease has a meaning for the person who suffers from it and for their environment. Suffering from a stomach ulcer, enteritis, high blood pressure, an inoperable carcinoma, or adult-onset diabetes, on the one hand, or suffering from a mental illness, on the other, are simply not the same thing. In the case of the former, the patient is usually met with a great deal of sympathy; in the case of the latter, the reaction may be dismay, rejection, reproach, or even accusation.

As a rule, we all suffer more from the meaning of the factum than from the factum itself (Musalek, 2003). The suffering arising from the meaning of an illness and the associated stigma is often greater than that caused by the symptoms. In any case, the importance ascribed to a specific pathological process, to being afflicted by a disease in the first place and to being sick is a fixed element in the conditional structure of our patients' suffering. Multidimensional diagnostics must therefore be oriented not only towards pathogenesis and process but also towards understanding (Musalek, 2003). The focus should not only be on symptoms but also on all the meanings the illness has for the individual and those who surround them. An understanding-oriented, differential diagnostic process, not limited to mental illness in the narrow sense, is indispensable when planning psychosocial and psychotherapeutic interventions. A deep understanding of the various meanings of the disease for all involved and insight into the disease on the part of the patient are needed if we are to overcome the relatively low level of adherence to treatment regimes, but this is often prevented by the narratives surrounding a particular disease (Musalek, 2003).

Conventional diagnostics mainly focus on the deficiencies brought about by the pathological process: symptoms, damage, impairments, disabilities, and handicaps. Multidimensional diagnostics cannot and must not be satisfied with merely listing deficiencies and understanding them through underlying processes and impacts on the life of the individual. It must always focus on the individual in his or her entire bodily and social existence. People afflicted with illness do not simply continue to exist in their illness; they also have healthy parts. As humans, we are never completely ill—even in the gravest illness, a residue of health is always preserved. Nor are we ever completely healthy: our body is always busy warding off abnormalities and pathogens. In other words, we are permanently living on a continuum between sickness and health, the fictitious extremes of which are "completely healthy" and "completely sick" (Musalek, 2010). In a differential diagnostic process, it is necessary to identify and seek out those parts of the person that are healthy and can be used as personal resources in treatment, with the goal of moving closer again to the (fictitious) pole of "completely healthy" on the health continuum.

Moreover, since the WHO defines health, the goal of treatment, not just as the absence of disease or infirmity but as a state of complete physical, mental, and social well-being, resource-oriented diagnostics becomes indispensable. This well-being, manifesting itself in a life that is as autonomous and happy as possible (Musalek, 2010), can only be achieved with full knowledge of the individual's positive strengths and resources in order to meaningfully employ them in the recovery process. Diagnostics that concerns itself with the human being as a whole, however, inevitably runs the risk of becoming lost in the imponderabilities of the human state of (not) knowing. Max Scheler showed quite plainly that man does not know "what he essentially is, but at the same time also knows that he does not know" (Scheler, 1929). Thus, even if we humans do not know (and will probably never be able to know) who we are, we are capable of forming a picture of ourselves and talking about ourselves. These images and narratives are not arbitrary figments of the imagination that simply have to be classified; they act as determining and driving forces in all of our lives. Resource-oriented diagnostics, focusing on the person as a whole, must be dedicated to these images and narratives we make of ourselves, even if here and there they are fragmented and sketchy.

The most prevalent concept of a human being in medicine today sees a whole person made up of more or less separate parts, such as the head, trunk, arms, legs, brain, reason, affects, drives, and so on. Seen as a whole, a person consists of spirit, soul, and psyche, on the one hand, and body, on the other. This "Two Worlds Story" (Ryle, 1949) is responsible for the dichotomous thinking currently so widespread in medicine: there are physical illnesses (diseases of the body) and mental illnesses (disorders of the psyche). Between the two, there are the so-called "psychosomatic" illnesses. However, this overlooks the fact that nowadays disorders are only regarded as psychiatric if they manifest themselves in psychological phenomena (this certainly should not be equated with having a psychological cause) and vice versa. Physical disorders are those that chiefly manifest themselves in physical symptoms (which again does not permit the conclusion that they only have physical causes). Furthermore, medicine based on the Two World's Story ignores the fact that a person is always a physical and a psychological being, including when they are suffering from an illness. Of course, sicknesses that have physical causes always impact on psychological life and experiences, and sicknesses with a psychological cause always affect the physical condition of the individual concerned. Seen from this perspective, all illnesses are psychosomatic—a point of view that modern psychosomatics has already made a central point of departure in research and application.

Human resources are characterised by a high degree of inter- and intra-individual variability. Resources are thus distributed extremely unevenly between individuals. What one person has at their disposal, another lacks—and vice versa. However, resources are not always uniformly available over a period of time: sometimes they are easy to use, and sometimes they move into the background, appear to have disappeared, and have to be brought to light again. Resources are not objects, life's spare tyre that can be used when life's tyre goes flat. They are processual happenings that need to be brought to life, strengthened and cultivated, made effective. The origin of the word "resource" draws attention to the fact that human resources are not merely skills that an individual can activate as needed, but are sources that, once they have been made to flow, can serve as genuine sources of strength. Such resources cannot be apprehended as intervariable and intravariable happenings in a single diagnostic act. This requires a differential diagnostic process that guides and accompanies the treatment of the person suffering from the psychological disorder. Only in this way can the potential of such resources be used to treat someone who is mentally ill as a whole person.

Firmly rooted in the tradition of the Two Worlds Story, the first resource-oriented approaches in medicine dealt with people's physical resources and with their psychological resources, with the latter divided into cognitive and affective resources. With growing social-psychiatric interest, the focus of attention was increasingly directed towards the bundle of social resources. We are familiar with financial, familial, professional resources, the resources derived from partnership and friendship, interactional resources, and with resources derived from social status and networks. Undoubtedly, the three main domains of personhood mentioned so far—the physical, psychological, and social—are important areas of strength. However, spiritual resources also constitute a special source of strength. Religious convictions, religious faith (of whatever kind) can release unbelievable strengths. However, people also possess a bundle of additional resources that can be divided into two groups: the group of "aesthetic resources" or "resources of beauty" and the group of "fictional resources" or "resources of the possible" (Musalek, 2012).

## Human-based medicine—patient management and treatment

To obtain all the knowledge about the patient and their sickness required in a differential diagnostic process and use it for therapeutic purposes in a pathogenic-oriented treatment plan, a deeper, more intense approach to sick people is required. Patient management is of central importance in the differential diagnostic and therapeutic processes. Traditional evidence-based medicine devotes little attention to the interaction between the patient and therapist; accordingly, there is a paucity of controlled studies in this area. Instead, effectiveness is attributed to the therapeutic agent, be it a psychopharmaceutical product or psychotherapeutic intervention. In his *Histoire de la folie* (1961), Michel Foucault bemoaned the "medical monologue" when the constitution of madness as a mental illness, at the end of the eighteenth century, affords the evidence of a broken dialogue. The language of psychiatry, which is a monologue of reason about madness, has been established only on the basis of such a silence. The constitution of mental illness in a postmodern medical world enables us to resume this broken dialogue with the other and his suffering (Musalek, 2003). It is no longer the monologue of the expert about the patient that determines the doctor–patient relationship. Only through genuine dialogue between doctor and patient can the patient be apprehended as a whole person, with all their potential, limitations, disorders, and resources. The goal of human-based medicine is that the therapist no longer superficially registers symptoms of disease with a view to creating the basis for an attempt at "symptom-killing" or making illness constructs disappear, but works with the patient to find new ways to enable them to find a way out of their suffering and to return to as autonomous and happy a life as possible.

This expression of a comprehensive state of well-being, as defined by WHO, is the most important treatment goal of human-based medicine. To achieve it, we have to move beyond a simple deficiency orientation to develop a resource-oriented treatment programme of the kind recently presented in Anton Proksch Institute's Orpheus Programme, a modular therapy programme for addicts based on attractive treatment objectives and a life that holds joy. Besides the usual physical, psychological, social, and spiritual resources, the main resources used in this programme are those of "beauty" and those of the possible (Musalek, 2010). Specially developed treatment modules, such as those on sensibility and sensitivity, awareness and mindfulness, body awareness, self-reflection, *Genussmodule* (pleasure and delight), and those enabling patients to experience nature and culture, seek to make the beautiful possible for the patient possible again and to enable them to find their way back to a life as self-determined and happy as possible.

Many people today still regard beauty as mere adornment, something that decorates life but is not really part of it, something that you can treat yourself to as a reward for having done what is essential in "real" life (the endured life). However, beauty is not just a special means of rewarding human tribulation; it is, above all, a tremendous source of strength (Musalek, 2012). How much strength do we have when we hike through beautiful mountain scenery and, by contrast, how little when we build strength on a home trainer? How much strength do we gain from a happy relationship? How much strength does a miserable one cost us? How much energy do we start what will be a lovely day for us? How listless do we seem on a day that promises to be unpleasant? How much vitality do we have doing work we enjoy? How strenuous is work we do not? And what about a lovely weekend or holiday as a source of relaxation and strength? The effects of beauty are direct and indirect, giving meaning and thus strength (Schmid, 2005). The beautiful is the quintessence of what is worth affirming. We all affirm the beautiful. Who in the world rejects from the bottom of their heart what is beautiful? Everything experienced as profoundly affirming is experienced as meaningful. Beauty gives meaning. We always question the meaning of our lives when we are no longer experiencing life as beautiful.

Beauty in our everyday lives can thus become a double source of strength. It is essential to enrich our daily lives with as much beauty as possible and not to regard beauty as a luxury we can only afford in small doses. The science that deals with beauty in everyday life, with the beauty of human togetherness and its impacts, is social aesthetics. Arnold Berleant (2005) regards it as an aesthetic of the situation. The most important tasks for social aesthetics in medicine are to cultivate interaction between the physician and the patient, fill empty rituals with humanity, create genuinely friendly atmospheres, deconstruct barriers, and open boundaries, to facilitate enjoyable (life) situations and reveal to the patient aesthetically agreeable perspectives for the future. This science is chiefly concerned with the scientific treatment of beauty in life spaces and atmospheres, in which the social development of life manifests itself, that is, life spaces and atmospheres that enable the individual to unfold their potential in a life that they find beautiful and the development of beautiful, and thus meaningful, social relationships (Musalek, 2010).

However, beauty should not be reduced to Apollonian beauty, a beauty that manifests itself in the balanced, the symmetrical, and the well proportioned. It is, above all, Dionysian beauty, whose phenomenology and force are brought home to us by Friedrich Nietzsche (1882) in his groundbreaking work *The Birth of Tragedy from the Spirit of Music*, which can serve as a tremendous source of strength. The exhilarating, enchanting, captivating, enthralling, and fascinating give us strength. To experience life as beautiful and appealing, we don't just need the Apollonian but also the Dionysian. A life without enchantment, without exhilaration, without enthusiasm and fascination, is a vapid life; it lacks something substantial that gives us vitality. However, the Apollonian and in particular the Dionysian can be counterproductive. The Apollonian loses its positive effect when overdosed: an excess of Apollonian beauty inevitably leads to anaesthesia. While the Dionysian does not lose its effect quite so quickly, it can, especially when Dionysian moments career out of control for long periods, result in moments that threaten the existence of the person caught up in the exhilaration. An uncontrolled surrender to the point of self-abandonment in the Dionysian inevitably leads to disaster. Dosage is therefore crucial when it comes to making optimal use of beauty as a source of strength. Learning how to correctly dose the Apollonian and Dionysian becomes one of life's central tasks—and not just for the sick!

The most effective resources for empowerment are, without a doubt, those of the possible. These resources, also known as fictional or optative resources, become visible and perceptible in the strengths that become available to us when we still believe that something is possible, when new opportunities offer themselves to us, when we are given options. They are also recognisable when we are robbed of the possible, when we no longer believe it is possible to achieve something, when opportunities are closed to us: loss of strength is the inevitable consequence. In his masterpiece, *The Man without Qualities*, Robert Musil (1978) describes a *Wirklichkeitsmensch*, who takes reality for what it is and creates with what is already there, and a *Möglichkeitsmensch*, whose focus is less on the real world and more on a world that is still possible. His main form of expression is not the indicative but the conjunctive: "it could be this way" instead of just "it is how it is". The *Möglichkeitsmensch* has a feeling for possible realities, for as yet unborn, presumptive realities. He lives his life focused on the utopian, on that which has not yet come into being. In an age like today, distinguished by a "strange shrinking of utopian consciousness" (Adorno, 1964), such possibility-charged individuals are often denigrated as fantasists, illusionists, or plain utopians. However, the possibility, the still possible, a yet unborn but already imagined reality are constitutive elements of further development. Without utopias, there will be no development of new realities.

A sense of reality and a sense of the possible are not irreconcilable; in their interaction as complementary sources of life, they enable us to reshape our world in a very special way. This chance mobilises our strengths; if it is denied us, we lose ourselves in powerlessness. This "not" as "not yet" is the breeding ground for our wishes. And the wishes generated can become the point of departure for our volition. Volition is a wish that has become action-effective: For a wish to become action-effective Bieri (2001) notes, one must have an idea of the steps that will lead to its fulfilment and have to develop the willingness to really take the necessary steps. Thus it is not enough to merely imagine the utopian. We are called on to identify what is possible for us and to mature feasible possibilities into a wish and to implement the wished as volition in goal-oriented actions. Making the possible possible is the central maxim of treatment.

The possible must not, however, be allowed to turn into unlimited possibilities. "Anything goes" (Feyerabend, 1975), so often and loudly proclaimed today, conceals the danger that everything that is in principle possible will be made impossible for the individual. In its claim to generality, the possible which is defined too widely and too broadly is experienced by the individual as being impossible (Bernegger, 2011). The all-embracing generally possible shows the individual in a special way everything that is impossible for them. Being forced to recognise that something that is generally possible—and thus possible for us—is after all not possible for us, always involves a loss of self-confidence. This is the reason why we no longer believe we are capable of doing anything, which results in a further loss of possibilities: a vicious circle. In a differential diagnostic process, it is essential to carefully define individual possibilities for a certain person in a certain situation, to seek them out, to uncover them, to make them visible, come alive, become achievable and realisable: making the possible possible. If we succeed, the individual can draw sufficient strength to successfully find paths out of the challenges they face in life and embark on those that enable them to again live a life as autonomous and happy as possible.

In contrast to strict evidence-based medicine, treatment based on the principles of human-based medicine is not focused solely on the "nature" of the disorder itself but to a considerable extent integrates the narratives surrounding the illness and the individual potential and limitations of the patient into the overall treatment plan. As basic personal resources required for treatment are not equally distributed among all patients, it is the task and art of the therapeutic team to fathom the potential and limitations of the individual patient and with them translate into action the resource-oriented treatment plan in an atmosphere of unqualified respect and warmth. This completes the step from a modern prescriptive medicine based on demands and instructions to a postmodern form based on dialogue.

Human-based medicine as outlined here is not an anti-pole to evidence-based medicine but can be perceived as an extension of the latter, It certainly does not rule out evidence-based approaches but integrates them into the treatment plan within a framework of dialogue on equal terms between therapist and patient. Evidence-based medicine as developed in our part of the world undoubtedly has great advantages: it opens up a host of excellent rational and efficient therapeutic possibilities and should not be abandoned. However, it needs to be complemented by a medicine in which it is no longer the disease construct but the person who is the measure of all things—a human-based medicine.

## References

Adorno, T. (1964). Radio interview von Ernst Bloch und Theodor Adorno zum Thema: Möglichkeiten der Utopien heute, aufgenommen. NDR. www.buecherkistze.org (accessed on 14 October 2012).

Audi, R. (1999). *The Cambridge Dictionary of Philosophy.* Cambridge: Cambridge University Press.

Berleant, A. (2005). Ideas for a social aesthetic. In: A. Light & J. M. Smith (Eds.), *The Aesthetics of Everyday Life.* New York: Columbia University Press.

Bernegger, G. (2011). Cited in M. Musalek (2012). Das Mögliche und das Schöne als Antwort. Neue Wege in der Burn-out-Behandlung. In: M. Musalek & M. Poltrum (Eds.), *Burnout: Glut und Asche.* Berlin: Parodos.

Bieri, P. (2001). *Das Handwerk der Freiheit.* München: Hanser.

Blackburn, S. (1996). *Dictionary of Philosophy.* Oxford: Oxford University Press.

Brockhaus (2004). *Der Brockhaus. Philosophie.* Mannheim: Brockhaus.

Buber, M. (1958). *I and Thou* (Trans. R. G. Smith). New York: Charles Scribner's Sons. (Reprinted from M. Buber, *Ich und Du*, Leipzig, 1923).

Feinstein, A. R. (1985). *Clinical Epidemiology: The Architecture of Clinical Research.* Philadelphia: Saunders.

Feyerabend, P. (1975). *Against Method.* New York: Verso, 2002.

Foucault, M. (1961). *Madness and Civilization: A History of Insanity in the Age of Reason.* New York: Random, 1988.

Heckmann, W., & Lotter, K. (2004). *Lexikon der Ästhetik* (2nd edn.). München: C. H. Beck.

Husserl, E. (1939). *Erfahrung und Urteil* (7th edn., Ed. L. von Landgrebe). Hamburg: Meiner, 1999.

Kramer, M. S. (1988). *Clinical Epidemiology and Biostatistics.* Berlin: Springer.

Kühlein, T., & Forster, J. (2007). Welche evidenz braucht der arzt? In: R. Kunz, G. Ollenschläger, & H. H. Raspe (Eds.), *Lehrbuch der Evidenzbasierten Medizin in Klinik und Praxis* (2nd edn.). Köln: Ärzteverlag.

Lyotard, J. -F. (1979). *La Condition Postmoderne.* Paris: Éditions Minuit.

Musalek, M. (2003). Meaning and causes of delusions. In: B. Fulford, J. Sadler, G. Stanghellini, & K. Morris (Eds.), *Nature and Narrative: International Perspectives in Philosophy and Psychiatry.* Oxford: Oxford University Press.

Musalek, M. (2004). Die Diagnose Sucht. Entwicklung des Suchtbegriffes, Diagnose, Kriterien. In: R. Brosch & R. Mader (Eds.), *Sucht-Problematik und Behandlung in Österreich* (p. 3). Vienna: LexisNexis.

Musalek, M. (2005). Unser therapeutisches Handeln im Spannungsfeld zwischen Warum und Wozu—Krankheitskonzepte und ihre

Auswirkungen auf die tägliche Praxis. *Wiener Zeitschrift für Suchtforschung* 3/4: 5–22.

Musalek, M. (2008). Neue Wege in der Diagnostik der Alkoholkrankheit: Von einer Defizienz-orientierten zur Ressourcen-orientierten Diagnostik. *Journal für Neurologie, Neurochirugie und Psychiatrie, 9(3)*: 46–52.

Musalek, M. (2010). Social aesthetics and the management of addiction. *Current Opinion in Psychiatry, 23*: 530–535.

Musalek, M. (2011). Evidenz-basierte Psychiatrie. Möglichkeiten und Grenzen. In: F. Schneider (Ed.), *Positionen der Psychiatrie*. Berlin: Springer.

Musalek, M. (2012). Das Mögliche und das Schöne als Antwort. Neue Wege in der Burn-out-Behandlung. In: M. Musalek & M. Poltrum (Eds.), *Burnout: Glut und Asche*. Berlin: Parodos.

Musil, R. (1978). *Der Mann ohne Eigenschaften*. Hamburg: Rowohlt.

Nestoriuc, Y., Kriston, L., & Rief, W. (2010). Meta-analysis as the score of evidence-based behavioral medicine: tools and pitfalls of a statistical approach. *Current Opinion in Psychiatry, 23*: 145–150.

Nietzsche, F. (1882). Die fröhliche Wissenschaft. In: G. Colli & M. Montinari (Eds.), *Friedrich Nietzsche Sämtliche Werke. Kritische Studienausgabe*. Berlin: De Gruyter, 1988.

Rohmann, C. (2001). *The Dictionary of Important Ideas and Thinkers*. London: Hutchinson Press.

Ryle, G. (1949). *Der Begriff des Geistes* (*The Concept of Mind*, Trans. K. Baier). Stuttgart: Reclam, 2002.

Sackett, D. L., Haynes, R. B., & Tugwell, P. (1985). *Clinical Epidemiology* (2nd edn.). Boston: Little, Brown & Co.

Sackett, D. L., Rosenberg, W. M. C., Muir, G. J. A., Haynes, R. B., & Richardson, W. S. (1996). Evidence-based medicine: what it is and what it isn't. *British Medical Journal, 312*: 71–72.

Scheler, M. (1929). *Die Stellung des Menschen im Kosmos*. Bonn: Bouvier, 2005.

Schischkoff, G. (1991). *Philosophisches Wörterbuch* (22nd edn.). Stuttgart: Alfred Kröner.

Schmid, W. (2005). *Schönes Leben? Einführung in die Lebenskunst*. Frankfurt/M: Suhrkamp.

Ulfig, A. (1999). *Lexikon der philosophischen Begriffe*. Wiesbaden: Marix.

Weiss, N. S. (1986). *Clinical Epidemiology: The Study of Outcome of Illness*. Oxford: Oxford University Press.

Wittgenstein, L. (1958). *Philosophical Investigations*. London: Prentice Hall.

World Health Organization (1993). *ICD-10: Classification of Mental and Behavioural Disorders*. Geneva: WHO.

# CHAPTER SEVEN

# Routes out of schizophrenia*

*Theodor Itten*

If we travel to St. Gallen in Switzerland by train, then, coming from the east, we emerge from the tunnel and pass first one set of points, then a second and a third, which determine at which platform we can alight. Or, if we know which direction the train will take from there, we can always remain seated. Some trains continue to Herisau, Rapperswil, and Lucerne; the stopping services dawdle on to Gossau and Wil. For the fast train to Zurich, Lausanne, or local trains for Teufen and Trogen, passengers are advised to change. Depending on what ideas we have about a journey, and the routes that can be taken out of "schizophrenia", we may choose one of the three platforms in the main station, or depart from the smaller branch-line station nearby.

What do we necessarily already recognise and acknowledge about the experience of, and insight into, a disorder that today I will call by a German name: *die geistige Zerrissenheit*—mental fragmentation? You

---

*This chapter is based on a talk "Wege aus der Schizophrenie" held in March 2012 for the "Vereinigung der Angehörigen von Schizophrenie-/Psychisch-Kranken" (VASK) in Switzerland. The original German presentation text was printed in the magazine *à jour!* published by the "Assoziation Schweizer Psychotherapeutinnen und Psychotherapeuten ASP" and translated for this chapter by Ruth Martin.

will all have known people who, in the past, or perhaps more recently, have received a psychiatric diagnosis of mental fragmentation—and have therefore also been affected yourselves. How do you—how do I—deal with these experiences, these phantasms, these labels?

Depending on the platform—the model of madness—depending on the set of points—the experience of mental disturbance—depending on the direction in which we travel—our tickets will take us on a journey through a particular (supposedly scientific) belief system. To paraphrase Andréa Belliger, Professor of Communication in Health Services at the University of Lucerne, patients are the experts on their own illness, and to shut them out of the treatment process is a simple waste of resources.

### Pauline Bleuler

Anna Pauline Bleuler (1852–1926), who was five years older than her psychiatrist brother, lived on the other side. She took paths that led off the beaten track, and her inner processes were turned outwards. She had broken down the bridges of sense and being connecting her to her brother Eugen (1857–1939) and her parents. In an attempt to shield her from a diagnosis of *dementia praecox* (premature senility, or mental enfeeblement in the young), which was then considered to be incurable, Eugen Bleuler described her condition using the metaphor of the broken or fractured heart—which, unfortunately, he translated into Greek. In the splitting of one's own being, we can sense a disharmony in physical, spiritual, and mental existence, which shows itself in a person's feelings, thoughts, experiences, desires, and actions. What we need, then, whether we are sick or/and not sick, disturbed or/and (according to the dimensional model of psychopathology) more or less undisturbed, is empathy, and a holistic consideration of our circumstances, which are all too frequently viewed as coincidental. The sister, having been diagnosed as catatonic, dumb, chronically ill, lived with the psychiatrist and his young family, in the maid's quarters. This arrangement was in keeping with Bleuler's understanding of the proximity involved in psychotherapy, which is an inner and outer therapeutic community of two people (or several, in a therapeutic community) in which one or the other is sick. In a therapeutic relationship, we investigate the origins of the suffering and the lack together, and what can be done—the "why" of the disorder—to make us well, whole again. In every case of illness, there is always a healthy life, which is often simply hidden within it.

## Holistic understanding

What we need today is a holistic understanding of mental illness that brings together research from sociology, psychology, biology, and cognitive sciences. Nothing, as we all know from our own lives, is monocausal, or true without its antithesis. So let us focus on the symptoms that point like route-markers to the issues that trouble us (mostly unconsciously), rather than labelling these symptoms with diagnoses, which for the most part simply stigmatise, and help nobody. The recent news about a "proven" schizophrenia gene will show itself for what it is: a false promise based on a misguided assumption, which is not valid in this case. Genes are overestimated: they are not a code or a "programme" for the form and behaviour of an organism. Genes determine the sequence of amino acids in protein molecules. A few are even involved in the control of protein synthesis. Since the conclusion of the Human Genome Project, which cost billions, and ran from 1990 until 2003, we can say for certain that there is no inherited schizophrenia gene. In the ETH laboratory for physiology and behaviour, Urs Meyer and his colleagues are investigating the influence of factors like infections and stress on the brain's development. Their hypothesis is that environmental influences like these encourage the emergence of so-called schizophrenia. The researchers are testing their theory using mice, rather than humans. Their aim is to develop drugs to combat the infection early on. It is clear that the more homogenously an academic group acts, the higher the probability that they are involved in a "lobby-economy" (Voss, 2013). Eugen's son, Manfred Bleuler (1903–1994), indicated this in a summary of his research on schizophrenia: "You know, ladies and gentlemen, although now and then we may have liked to simplify it, complex life relationships cannot be solved through a reduction of complexity" (1984, p. 143).

## Language

What kind of words do we use to talk about this phenomenon (that is, what is not hidden; what we can observe), of spiritual and mental fragmentation, each experience of which is unique—and what sense, what meaning do we ascribe to them?

In everyday speech, we might say that a person is "mad".[1] The word has been in use since the late thirteenth century, and is synonymous with the phrase "out of one's mind"—living at a remove from logic and sense. "Crazy" comes from the 1570s, and means "full of cracks and flaws"—fragmented, in other words. The term "schizophrenia"— mental schism, split consciousness—comes from the Greek *schizein*: to split, divide, cut, dissolve. Its second half comes from the Greek *phren*: intellect, mind, diaphragm.

Why am I unpicking these words that we use to describe and discuss, note and name, the experience of mental disorders? So that on the platforms we can understand each other to some degree. Otherwise we will go "off the rails", and miss each other. The Greek word *diagnose* means to discern, to get a perspective. A *prognosis* is a prediction, and also means foreknowledge, which we cannot have in this matter. We class something as a psychotic episode, if a psychiatric expert calls into question a person's subjective experience and reflective competence. Or if a person (mostly the future patient) misinterprets and misunderstands the reality that we share in normal everyday life. If in another world, I should believe that I am Napoleon and not just Itten, then you can regard me, for the time being, as mad. Perhaps I feel within myself the dilemma between need—the need for validation—and fear. In 1969, various doctors and psychotherapists published their experience of this dilemma in relation to schizophrenia (Burnham et al., 1969).

One of the psychologists currently leading the way on mental health and mental illness is Richard Bentall, Professor of Clinical Psychology at the University of Liverpool. His most recent book, entitled *Doctoring the Mind: Is Our Current Treatment of Mental Illness Really Any Good?* was published in 2009. The book casts a critical eye over the majority of contemporary research, and various forms of therapy, including routes out of mental fragmentation. He says: "Even the most deluded patients are able to think rationally about matters unrelated to their delusional beliefs" (2009, p. 279). And: "It is difficult to know how many psychotic patients would be better off without taking drugs, but my guess is that the number might be as high as 50 per cent" (p. 282). And in the area of the well-being economy: recovering from psychoses is generally easier when economic conditions are favourable. It is easier to find meaning in life, independence, a sense of self-worth and self-confidence, when there is plenty of work around, and harder when unemployment is high. The total survival time is an important factor in measuring health. And this, as current research shows, is dramatically reduced when someone is on permanent medication. This empirical evidence and more is provided by the second edition of *Models of Madness* (Read & Dillon, 2013) which shows the various entry points to psychosis. In *Patient im Visier, die neue Strategie der Pharmakonzerne*, Walter and Kobylinski (2011) point out the shocking fact that hardly anybody is conducting truly patient-oriented research. Their conclusion is that health policy has failed: politicians are allowing pharmaceutical companies to go on making billions in profits, while perpetuating the suffering of ill people.

Years ago, a pianist came to see me, wanting to discuss his thoughts about death. He had been surprised to discover that, for a forthcoming concert, all he could think of were songs for the dead. He wondered whether he might be experiencing a mental disorder, a psychotic episode? Later, he started to have suicidal thoughts and was admitted to a psychiatric hospital. There, he was given the provisional diagnosis that he was suffering from a psychotic episode. Having been for a walk in the town, he was unable to find his way back to the clinic. He asked somebody, and was given directions to the main hospital. When he arrived there, now confused, he was given a neurological examination. They discovered two huge brain tumours, the symptoms of which had manifested as organic psychosis. This is in contrast to functional psychosis—mental fragmentation, which can manifest itself in various moods: on top of the world one minute, in the depths of despair the next; withdrawal and dejection; persecution complexes; anxiety; inner voices; inner choruses; megalomania. When somebody experiences the world in an extraordinary way, their perception leads to behaviours that make the other an Other. As parents, relatives, friends, and experts, you will be familiar with these experiences in all their variety. You have all worried about and cared for your relatives, you have reached the limits of the care you could give. You gave as much sympathy as they could stand. For me, as a psychotherapist, symptoms are metaphors that, like timetables or the information on street signs, can show us where to go. They are emotional, corporeal reactions to adverse, often frightening, life events.

## The platforms of madness

The aforementioned train station in St. Gallen has five platforms to choose from. For this analogy, I will call

Platform One: somatic medicine
Platform Two: depth-psychology
Platform Three: systematic communication
Platform Four: social psychology
Platform Five: psychosocial politics—society and family.

As you can see, the entire range is served there: body, mind, spirit, as well as transpersonal and social aspects of our selves. And depending on which platform you and I embark from, our journey will take us in a specific direction, determining the route we can take out of mental fragmentation. Along the way, we can interpret the great wounds from childhood and from the present time, using interpretive paradigms, conditioned by theories and their explanatory models.

### Platform One: somatic medicine

Humanity has practised psychopharmacology for thousands of years—probably about four thousand years. Alcohol, opium, marijuana, and other healing herbs were the first drugs to be discovered and used. We use mild substances every day: coffee, nicotine, amphetamines. With the discovery in the 1950s of benzodiazepine (valium) for anxiety, and chlorpromazine for confused thinking, and the confusion of hallucinations and reality, the fast train started picking up speed. But unfortunately, as commonly experienced by such patients, chemical remedies do not alleviate mental problems. We now have another puzzle to solve—namely, how the drugs work on the brain and how the brain chemistry is altered. There are a great many assumptions about and models of these effects available, especially in the chemical industry's advertising brochures. Synapse modelling, chemical transfer balance, genetic inheritance and predispositions—all the way to the "schizophrenia gene". All these are simply temporary working definitions, put forward in order to secure funding for further research. Manfred Bleuler often cited the fact that around twenty percent of schizophrenic psychoses are cured by psychotic or neuroleptic remedies, but the percentage take a disastrous course in spite of administering neuroleptic drugs.

I just read another outrageous claim in the *St. Galler Tagblatt* newspaper (2012) about schizophrenia being heritable, before mentioning that researchers have been unable to identify any responsible gene. This is all just about power, pharmaceutical industry machinations, and a lot of money for research from the public purse. In *pms aktuell* (Rudolf, 2012), the journal of Pro Mente Sana, I discovered a report on something I didn't know existed—Jansen-Cilag's "schizophrenia simulator", a multi-media installation in a truck, called "Paved with Fear". The aim is to give people who have never had any kind of psychosis a first-hand experience of "what their schizophrenia patients endure every day". Gaby Rudolf, a writer for *pms*, visited the "Fear Truck" with three people who had experience of psychosis (among others), and came to the conclusion that after experiencing this project, it is impossible to talk impartially about schizophrenia. The visitors described schizophrenia as the purest horror.

The term "schizophrenia" has been in use for a good hundred years. In the UK, the Schizophrenia Commission (2012), chaired by Professor Robin Murray and comprised of fourteen independent experts, spent a year investigating the meaning, purpose, and usage of this concept, and the various treatment systems in the UK. They discovered that treatment based on the biological model of madness was demoralising, which had an unwholesome effect on the healthy aspects of a patient's mind. This is clearly unacceptable for the UK in the twenty-first century. The report calls for an end to diagnoses of schizophrenia, so that today mental suffering in the population can be treated more seriously again. In the report, psychotherapy is viewed as very helpful for people suffering psychotic episodes. In one of the commission's surveys, on the wider use of the concept of schizophrenia, over eighty percent of respondents gave answers to the effect that this diagnosis has an injurious and destructive effect.

*Platforms Two and Three: depth-psychology, systematic communication*

In various publications on the topic of *The Divided Self*, the title of his first book, Ronald D. Laing (1927–1989) tried to relax the tense situation that exists between psychiatrist and patient. As early as the 1950s, he wrote how important it is for us as professionals to consider that it would be a fallacy to say: "we know what's going on, but the patient doesn't".[2]

"I think, however that schizophrenics have more to teach psychiatrists about the inner world than psychiatrists their patients" (Laing, 1967, p. 91). A person who is undergoing a psychotic episode often gives us, the people on the outside, the feeling that they are "not letting the sounds of the world penetrate their being", as Siegfried Lenz so beautifully put it. At the start of his book *The Divided Self* (1960), Laing (who wrote this book between the ages of twenty-five and twenty-eight) says:

> The term schizoid refers to an individual the totality of whose expe-
> rience is split in two main ways: in the first place, there is a rent in
> his relation with his world and, in the second, there is a disruption
> of his relation with himself. Such a person is not able to experience
> himself "together with" others or "at home in" the world, but, on
> the contrary, he experiences himself in despairing aloneness and
> isolation; moreover, he does not experience himself as a complete
> person but rather as "split" in various ways, perhaps as a mind
> more or less tenuously linked to a body, as two or more selves, and
> so on. (p. 15)

When he wrote this book, Laing was the same age as Emil Kraeplin (1856–1926) when he wrote his *Psychiatry Textbook*, in which he devel-oped the concept of *dementia praecox*. Do twenty-eight-year-old psychi-atrists have a particular need to draw attention to themselves at this precise age? Eugen Bleuler, for his part, was the first Swiss psychiatrist to bring Sigmund Freud's psychoanalysis to "his" Burghölzli psychiat-ric hospital at the University of Zurich, and practise it there. For him, emotional ambivalence was one of the principal symptoms suggesting somebody was suffering *a fragmented heart*. As mentioned above, his own sister was on the other side of normal. In my view, he was try-ing to protect her using this metaphor of the fragmented heart. This ambivalence, I believe, is commonly visible with regard to inner and outer worlds. The bridge of behaviour determines what I let out from inside. From the outer world, issues come into me, whether permitted or unpermitted. Sometimes the bridges are pulled up, and the inner and outer banks of life are temporarily disconnected. We use concepts such as silence, peace, emptiness, or respite for this mental disposition. I often imagine what would have happened if Bleuler had not used a Greek word for his protective concept, but called it the "broken or fragmented heart". Our forebears might have realised that mental suf-fering, melancholy, and anguish constitute part of life. The medical and psychiatric sciences would not have had to conduct a hundred years of pointless research (except in the view of the pharmaceutical industry, which has seen huge financial gains). Many people's lives would not have been made needlessly harder, with sometimes irreparable damage caused by psychotropic drugs, electric shocks, or other failed treatments, depending on the period. Numerous publications from around the world, from organisations of people who have undergone psychiatric treatment, bear witness to this.

Laing's study on the divided self provided the foundation for his social and existential phenomenology, in which he tried to describe the nature of a person's experience of the world and themselves. His goal was to recognise the way we see people's "being in the world", our gaze—our diagnosis (perspective)—for what it is: a view conditioned by textbooks and training, socialisation. In psychiatry, this diagnostic gaze is trained using particular textbooks and tenets. Our sense and understanding of others come from considering the people who seek our help as psychotherapists, and listening to what they tell us about their lives. We consider the behaviour of others, which turns it into our experience. The way I experience others informs my behaviour towards them. Interpersonal phenomenology moves away from the image of sickness, and looks at the lived-in world within which mental suffering arises. We investigate the *sense* of the suffering. We live, and are being lived, sometimes at the mercy of our unconscious. A large meta-analysis by Asay and Lambert (1999) investigating common factors in modern psychotherapy showed the following empirical evidence of what works across all forms of therapy:

- Methods and concept factors: fifteen percent
- Expectations and placebo effects: fifteen percent
- Psychotherapeutic relationship: thirty percent
- Patient factors and extra-therapeutic changes: forty percent.

What do these results mean for patients and for psychotherapists? The change that leads to healing lies in the interaction between the people, since it is not the people in themselves who change. Whether we are practising psychotherapy, cognitive behavioural therapy, psychoanalysis, or body psychotherapy plays only a secondary role. The most important things in psychotherapy are the therapeutic relationship and life context and education of the patient. What is divided really belongs together. We have all the dualities of inner and outer, private and public, being and not-being, true and false, and so on. We speak of mindfulness versus loneliness. In Switzerland, this treatment model is well known, through the Soteria in Bern. The institute was conceived and turned into a success by the social psychiatrist Luc Ciompi, who modelled it on Loren Mosher's Soteria California.[3]

*Platform Four: community psychology*

Researchers at the University Medical Center Hamburg-Eppendorf use the "treatment conference", a systemic family therapy based on genealogical family trees, as a model of integrative care. Their research (Aderhold, Gottwalz, & Haßlöwer, 2010; Aderhold & Gottwalz-Itten, 2013; Bock, 1997) demonstrates that optimised outpatient treatment using person-centred therapy gives better results than the standard care route taken from Platform One. In this model, relatives can come to recognise that what the temporarily disturbed and disturbing person in their midst says, makes more sense in the context of the family and its trans-generational issues than is usually assumed. A study with over a hundred families that Laing and Esterson conducted in London from 1959 to 1964 showed similar results fifty years ago (Laing & Esterson, 1964). Finding the route out of the constriction of being disturbed, and moving towards becoming healed and whole again, stands at the centre of this guided process. "What's this all for?" can be a question that opens up a past experience to the present and future. In many cases, says a report in the Hamburger Abendblatt (2013), it appears connected with a particular development, finding one's own path in life, generally under particularly severe conditions of inner and outer disharmony, and sometimes (in almost a quarter of cases) the trauma of abuse (violent, sexual, emotional). There is frequently an initial loss, when the confrontation between a person's inner world and outer reality (true self and false self system) is given up. Finding personal unity in their own social being is difficult, and it is so painful to recognise how far out of life they have fallen that they reach an "I can't go on" moment.

*Platform Five: psychosocial politics and culture*

From Manfred Bleuler's family, and his longitudinal study we know—and this has not been disproved to this day—that one-third of people who become ill and suffer with mental fragmentation make a full recovery without treatment; one-third get better with the aid of psychotherapy, and sometimes short courses of low-dose medication; and, unfortunately, one-third often remain chronically ill. No researcher has yet been able to tell us exactly why this is. Thomas Bock, a professor of psychology in Hamburg, investigated psychoses without psychiatry in his book *Lichtjahre* ("light-years"). The 1997 study, which was his *habilitation* thesis, documents how people with untreated psychoses understand their illnesses and plan to live their lives. In 1989, together with Dorothea Buck, he set up the first psychosis seminar in Hamburg. These seminars, a trialogue between sufferers, relatives, and people working in psychiatry, are now very well established there. Buck's own report (1994), *Auf der Spur des Morgensterns—Psychose als Selbstfindung* (On the Trail of the Morning Star, Psychosis as Self-Discovery)—is legendary. Lehmann and Stastny tried something similar in their anthology *Alternatives Beyond Psychiatry* (2007). This book contains stories from self-help groups for people who have experienced psychoses, and who help each other through them, without psychiatric institutions. In his concluding remarks to the Swiss Society for Psychiatry's annual conference in September 1983, the theme of which was schizophrenia, Manfred Bleuler (1983, p. 149) wrote: "We see a schizophrenic as one of us, who in the battle for a self, a personal existence, in which we are all engaged, has given up in exhaustion, and has stopped making his inner contradictions conform to reality."

Psychotherapy is, of course, an intense spiritual and emotional interaction. At the same time, in these deliberations and debates, as we compare platforms, ponder destinations, consider the various possibilities for being human, and the 13.81 million years since the Big Bang (according to a recent estimate, with a margin for error of 50 million years), I always think of Hans Vaihinger's philosophy of the "as if", in which he looks at how we often reach correct conclusions using consciously false assumptions.

Vaihinger's (1911) philosophy proposed that man willingly accept falsehoods or fictions in order to live peacefully in an irrational world. Vaihinger, who saw life as a maze of contradictions and philosophy as a search for means that made life liveable, embraced Immanuel Kant's view that knowledge is limited to phenomena and cannot extend to things-in-themselves. In order to flourish, man must wilfully construct convenient explanations for phenomena "as if" there were rational grounds for believing that such a method was sound. Logical contradictions were best disregarded. Thus in physics, man must proceed "as if" a material world exists independently of perceiving subjects; in behaviour, he must act "as if" ethical certainty were possible; in religion, he must believe "as if" there were a God.

### Before the train departs

Psychosocial interventions—and there is empirical evidence of this (Read & Dillon, 2013)—are better suited to treating mental disorders and suffering in a safe way, without causing injury, than the medicinal, pharmacological variety. When the mind suffers, it needs a change of track, away from the pessimistic ideology promoted by biological psychiatry and the chemical industry, towards a humane approach to the healing arts like that of Aeschylus, practised for thousands of years, but which is also modern and evidence-based. To finish, a few lines from a poem by Kurt Marti (1971):

> The heaven that is, is not the heaven to come, when heaven and earth
> are gone away.
> The heaven to come is the world without pain, with violence and
> misery defeated.
> The heaven to come is the joyful city and God with a human face.
> The heaven to come will greet the earth that is here, when life is
> transformed by love.

### Notes

1. The German term here is *verrückt*, which also means "to be moved (*rücken*) from a place". *Wahn* is also commonplace—the meaning is similar to the English "mania". It comes from the eighth century, and the Middle High German *wan*: hope, expectation; and *wen*: endeavour, hope. *Wahn* is often used to mean empty, ignorant, lacking. It can also mean taking another path.
2. "The personal human approach he preached as if his own permeated the Scottish School as I knew it", so says Isobel Hunter-Brown (2007, p. 28).
3. Aebi, Ciompi, Hansen (1993); Ciompi, Hoffmann, Broccard (2001).

## References

Aderhold, V., Gottwalz, E., & Haßlöwer, H. (2010). Die Behandlungskonferenz—Dialog, Reflexion und Transparenz. *Psychiatrische Pflege Heute, 16*: 142–152.

Aderhold, V., Gottwalz-Itten, E. (2013). Family therapy and psychosis—replacing ideology with openness. In: J. Read & J. Dillon (Eds.), *Models of Madness* (2nd edn.; pp. 378–391). London: Routledge.

Aebi, E., Ciompi, L., & Hansen, H. (Eds.) (1993). *Soteria im Gespräch*. Bonn: Psychiatrie Verlag.

Asay, T. P., & Lambert, M. J. (1999). The empirical case for the common factors in therapy: quantitative findings. In: M. A. Hubble, B. L. Duncan, & S. D. Miller (Eds.), *The Heart and the Soul of Change: What Works in Therapy?* (pp. 33–56). Washington, DC: APA Books.

Bentall, R. P. (2009). *Is Our Current Treatment of Mental Illness Really Any Good?* New York: New York University Press.

Bleuler, M. (1983). Closing remarks. Swiss Society for Psychiatry's Annual Conference Report. *Schweizer Archiv für Neurochirurgie und Psychiatrie, 135(1)*: 143–149.

Bleuler, M. (1984). Das alte und das neue Bild der Schizophrenen [translated for this edition]. *Schweizer Archiv für Neurologie, Neurochirurgie, Psychiatrie, 135*: 143–149.

Bock, T. (1997). *Lichtjahre—Psychosen ohne Psychiatrie*. Köln: Psychiatrie Verlag.

Buck, D. (1994). *Auf der Spur des Morgensterns—Psychose als Selbstfindung*. Berlin: List.

Burnham, D. L., Gladstone, A. I., & Gibson, R. W. (1969). *Schizophrenia and the Need–Fear Dilemma*. New York: New York University Press.

Ciompi, L., Hoffmann, H., & Broccard, M. (2001). *Wie wirkt Soteria?* Bern: Huber.

Hamburger Abendblatt (2013). UKE: Schizophrenia: when the soul suffers. 23/24.3.2013.

Hunter-Brown, I. (2007). *R. D. Laing and Psychodynamic Psychiatry in 1950's Glasgow: A Reappraisal*. London: Free Association.

Laing, R. D. (1967). *The Politics of Experience*. London: Penguin.

Laing, R. D., & Esterson, A. (1964). *Sanity, Madness and the Family*. Vol. I: *Families of Schizophrenics*. London: Tavistock Publications.

Marti, K. (1971). Der Himmel, der ist [translated for this edition]. In: *Republikanische Gedichte* (new edn.). Neuwied: Luchterhand.

Mosher, L. R., & Hendrix, V. (2004). *Soteria*. Bloomington, IN: Xlibris.

Read, J., & Dillon, J. (Eds.) (2013). *Models of Madness* (2nd edn.). London: Routledge.

Rudolf, G. (2012). Fear truck. In: *Pms aktuell, 1*: 32.

Schizophrenia Commission (2012). *The Abandoned Illness*. London: Rethink Mental Illness    www.schizophreniacommission.org.uk/the-report (Accessed 30 August 2014).

St. Galler Tagblatt (2012). Raucher werden leichter Schizophren—Studie der Uni Zürich und Köln. *St. Galler Tagblatt*, 27 March.

Stastny, P., & Lehmann, P. (Eds.) (2007). *Alternatives Beyond Psychiatry*. Berlin: Peter Lehmann.

Vaihinger, H. (1911). *Die Philosophie des Als Ob*. Aalen: Scientia, 1986.

Voss, J. (2013). Steinzeit für immer. *Frankfurter Allgemeine Zeitung*, 25 March.

Walter, C., & Kobylinski, A. (2011). *Patient im Visier, die neue Strategie der Pharmakonzerne*. Berlin: Suhrkamp.

# CHAPTER EIGHT

# Counting the cost

*Claire Entwistle*

After years of neglect, "talking therapies" are both in demand and in short supply in the British National Health Service (NHS), the new market being dominated by Cognitive Behaviour Therapy and other short-term focused techniques. At the same time, there are many private and public institutions training psychotherapists for in-depth, long-term work which NHS commissioners are unlikely to fund. Most are training at their own expense. In this chapter, I explore the motivations and commitment of this group who are expending considerable financial and other resources to train and practice in what might seem to be an inhospitable climate.

I became interested in this questions when I realised recently that I knew, in contexts unrelated to my clinical work, a surprising number of people who are training as psychotherapists or psychotherapeutic counsellors. Weekly personal therapy is required at least until the practitioner is qualified, and unpaid placements are often compulsory, with supervision that may be paid for by the student. All in all, these trainings are very expensive and time-consuming, as well as emotionally demanding.

When the builder mentioned that he was paying £140 per week just to cover the supervision for his voluntary placements, I wondered how much the training was costing him in total, and how long it would be before he earned enough from practising as a psychotherapist even to cover his outlay. In fact, how easy would it be for him, or any of these trainees, to find any paid work after qualifying? There is no clear answer to this question, but the situation does not look particularly promising in Britain. UKCP survey data from 2012 shows that the majority of psychotherapists work in private practice, but it is notoriously slow to set up in this way, and the UKCP and BACP registers suggest that competition is heavy in most parts of the country. Some paid posts exist in charities, colleges, and so on; these are advertised in the professional journals, but it is notable that there are usually only a handful of such vacancies in each issue, alongside pages of advertisements for trainings, MAs, CPD, and supervision: in other words, services that support existing therapists or create new ones. Looking at this imbalance, and taking into account the fact that trainee psychotherapists have to be in individual psychotherapy right through their training period, one may wonder whether psychotherapists are mostly working for each other, rather than for the general public.

In theory, there are alternatives to setting up a private practice. In Britain, the NHS increasingly offers short-term counselling in GP surgeries and hospitals, as well as some longer-term work. Psychotherapists trained at independent centres are qualified to do this, but they come into competition with professionals in other fields, such as nurses or social workers who have been trained in cognitive analytic therapy (CAT) or systemic family therapy. Such roles are also increasingly filled by volunteers on extended placements.

I was curious to notice, when talking with the trainee psychotherapists I know, that although they enjoyed discussing their courses and the importance of psychotherapy in their own lives, and sometimes mentioned that some aspect of the training was expensive, nobody spoke about how much they hoped eventually to be earning after they qualified, or expressed much concern about the likelihood or otherwise of finding paid work. These were all successful professionals in other fields, but they did not appear to have even a back of the envelope business plan for their career change.

I began to wonder how common these attitudes were, but there seemed to be little research data available on the questions that particularly interested me: how much, on average, were these trainee psychotherapists actually spending on training, and how much work did they expect to be doing after qualifying? How long did they expect it would take even to earn back the amount they had spent on their training? How did they *feel* about making this outlay, and how did they expect to feel about it later when they started working with paying clients? Was it possible that their desire to work as psychotherapists was so strong that the financial implications were almost irrelevant?

## The research study

I will briefly describe the format and results of a small research study I conducted to throw some light on these questions, using semi-structured interviews and an online survey to ask both trainees and established psychotherapists for their thoughts about money and motivation (Entwistle, 2013). Please see the reference below for the link to an online version of the full survey results.

First, I interviewed four people, two currently in psychotherapy training and two who had recently qualified. I asked them to talk freely about the cost of their training, how much they expected to earn in the first few years after qualifying, how they came to choose psychotherapy rather than any alternatives they might have considered, and how they felt about the financial aspects of their choice.

Next I used their responses as the basis for an online survey aimed at a wider group. I listed a number of statements made by the interviewees, with tick boxes where the survey respondents could indicate whether they agreed or disagreed with each statement, with the option to leave the tick box blank if they neither agreed nor disagreed.

The survey was distributed via email groups in the UK. Sixty complete responses were collected, thirty-five from "Qualified" and twenty-five from "Trainee" respondents.

## The questions and responses

### What were the costs?

I started the face-to-face interviews by asking the four participants to estimate the amount they had spent, or expected to spend, on their training and on the unavoidable extra expenses—personal therapy, supervision for placement sessions, travel, and so on. The interviewees estimated that their training fees cost between £5,000 and £15,000, and that the additional expenses cost about the same amount again.

The same question was included in the online survey. Survey respondents came from several different modalities, and this was reflected in the range of training costs. The "Trainee" group included students on a two-year course at a local college who were paying just £3,000, whilst another respondent, who was completing her second training, had paid a total of £40,000 in fees. The median cost of fees for the "Trainee" group was £15,000.

The additional cost quoted by the "Trainees" varied even more wide-ranging, lying between £3,000 and £65,000, with a median of £10,500. Certain comments in the free-text sections of the survey, it seemed gave the impression that some respondents had included a figure to represent earnings from paid work lost as a direct result of attending their training, though strictly these should have been shown separately as "opportunity costs".

Adding together the median training fees and the median "additional costs", the current cost of training as a psychotherapist in Britain today appears to be around £25,500.

*Had they calculated this cost before taking on the training, and how did they feel about it?*

The responses from my interviewees to my second question—whether they had calculated the cost before starting their training, and what were their feelings about it—yielded some illuminating comments, which I shall describe in some detail.

The first interviewee, whom I will call Sam, said that she had calculated the cost and felt she could afford it. Sam had worked as a psychotherapist many years ago and wanted to "refresh" her training. She understood the economics of the psychotherapy world and had saved enough to cover the fees and extra expenses. She was keen to get back to working as a psychotherapist and felt happy to spend her money in this way.

The second interviewee, Chris, was part-way through her training and had a rough idea how much it would cost in total. She had had to borrow the funds from various relatives and said she was not comfortable about this, particularly since her parents had helped her financially during university. "My parents made sacrifices to make sure I got a good education and a good start in my career, and now here I am start-ing again and incurring debts."

The other two interviewees, Finn and Dale, had both committed to do the training without working out the total cost. Finn's parents had contributed to the first stage and she was not sure how she was going to fund the remaining years, except perhaps by borrowing, taking on extra freelance work, or selling her possessions, including some with sentimental value.

Dale, who had recently qualified, said: "I never added it up. When I started the course, I did not think about the professional side, or how much it would cost to do, or how much I would make after qualifying. I just felt compelled to do it. It was the same when I started personal therapy. Could I afford that? No! I had a badly paid job and was rent-ing an expensive flat at the time, and I was single." However, Dale did have moments of resentment towards the end of her training, when she started working in placements: "It was only when I started in the vol-untary placements that I got resentful and realised what the financial and time commitment really was. I was not resentful against the clients but with the organisations. They were happy to waste my time but they were very demanding of me." Dale was in fact very reluctant to know exactly how much she had spent, and only agreed to add it up during the interview.

These sentiments—concern about the cost and reluctance to calcu-late it—were reflected in similar proportions in the survey:

- Fewer than half (forty-eight per cent) of the respondents had worked out the cost of the fees plus the additional expenses in advance.
- Well over half (sixty-two per cent) said they felt "concerned" about the amount of money they were spending, and one used the term "eye-watering".
- The majority (fifty-five per cent of the "Qualified" psychotherapists and 76% of the "Trainee" group) said they had "borrowed money or made significant sacrifices" to train.

During the interviews and in the survey, nobody suggested that they could comfortably afford their training, though a few mentioned cir-cumstances that had helped them, including a rent-free spell abroad, a husband who offered support, and an inheritance.

*How much did they expect to earn?*

The interviewees spoke with varying degrees of confidence about how much they expected to earn as psychotherapists. Sam and Chris both acknowledged that they would face a lot of competition, but felt optimistic about reaching the goals they had set themselves. Sam hoped eventually to make around £10,000 per annum from seeing clients part-time, but expected to take a while to reach this level. Chris hoped to earn around £30,000 per annum from therapy-related work once she was established. She expected this to be challenging but had confidence in her own motivation: "I believe that some things work out. On paper it may not make sense, but I care about this so much that I believe I will succeed."

Finn had not thought about how much she might eventually earn, but said she hoped to spend about one-third of her working hours seeing clients. Dale, who had also given little thought to her eventual earnings, had been qualified for a year at the time of the interview, and so far had earned a few hundred pounds.

*How long to recoup the cost of their training?*

None of the interviewees volunteered a comparison between the amount they were spending on their training and their expected earnings. When asked, they all reckoned that it would be "several years" before they earned enough to cover the cost of their training.

In the survey, the "Trainee" respondents were invited to say whether they expected to make back the cost of their training "in the first few years" of working as psychotherapists. Only eighteen per cent of them said that they expected this. Of the "Qualified" group, a slightly higher proportion (twenty-three per cent) estimated that they had in fact covered the costs, and so had begun to see a profit, "in the first few years".

*How did they feel about the economics of psychotherapy training?*

None of the interviewees had ever thought in terms of how long it would take to earn enough from their psychotherapy work to cover the costs of the training, and there was some consternation when they attempted to estimate this during the interviews. Nobody said that this realisation made them regret taking their new direction, although one interviewee mentioned a few weeks later that she was considering for the first time whether she could afford to complete her training. The interviewees all spoke of the personal value of the training irrespective of their eventual earnings. A typical comment from Chris: "Of course I want to make some money from therapy, but the training was well worth it anyway in terms of my personal development."

Three of the four interviewees went further and stated that they would seriously consider working for nothing if they could not find paid work. The survey included a statement "the money I am spending on the training is worth it in terms of my personal development even if I don't make much money from working as a therapist". Forty per cent of the "Trainee" group and sixty-five per cent of the "Qualified" psychotherapists agreed with this statement.

*Were they motivated by their experience of being a client?*

Working with clients was clearly important to some of these psycho-therapists on a personal as well as a professional level. In what ways? Three of the interviewees volunteered that their experience of receiving therapy was a significant factor in wanting to work as psychothera-pists themselves; they had been clients for a while and did not want to lose the experience of relating in this way when the time came to finish. As Finn put it, "it seemed like a natural continuation of the work, to become a psychotherapist myself".

These sentiments were reflected in the survey:

- The statement "my own experience as a client was a significant fac-tor in choosing psychotherapy as a profession" was agreed with by sixty-five per cent of "Qualified" and fifty-five per cent of "Trainee" participants.
- The same proportions agreed with the statement "Being in therapy as a client has been one of the most important things in my life"; this was also ticked by sixty-five per cent of "Qualified" and fifty-five of "Trainee" respondents.
- Even more frequently ticked was the statement "Being in therapy as a client has changed my life for the better", being ticked by seventy-seven per cent of the "Qualified" psychotherapists and eighty-one per cent of the "Trainees".

- An opportunity to express less positive feelings was offered by two statements in the survey:

  ○ "I sometimes wonder if psychotherapy/counselling really helps people." This was agreed with by twenty-one per cent of "Qualified" psychotherapists and thirty-two per cent of "Trainees".
  ○ "I had to undergo personal therapy as a part of my training, but otherwise I might not have chosen to have therapy myself." Just seventeen per cent of the "Qualified" psychotherapists agreed with this, and a more substantial forty-one per cent of the "Trainees".

This last point, showing that a significant minority of the current trainees in the survey started their training without being, or wanting to be, in therapy themselves, suggests that for some trainees the experience of being a client was *not* an important factor in deciding to become a psychotherapist, and that their enthusiasm for being on the receiving end of therapy grew with the experience.

Some of the feeling behind these positive statements was clarified in the interviews and the survey free text comments:

- "It was a way of continuing the kind of relationship that I had with my own therapist; it didn't seem to matter much what side of the conversation I was on."
- "Having had a brief experience as a client, I just knew that I wanted to be a counsellor—then, a psychotherapist—and help others the way in which I had been enabled to express feelings and thoughts which had not come out before, or for a very long time."
- "The time came to finish my therapy; in a way I was ready to leave, and I thought, why would I want to give this up? It's wonderful."

## What was it about psychotherapy that attracted them?

What was so "wonderful" about psychotherapy? Three of the four interviewees mentioned, unprompted, that they wanted to offer something different from "treatments" or "the medical model". They were not attracted to the prospect of "removing" problems, but wanted to look for meaning within them. As Dale put it: "Pain is valuable, and we need to learn to live with it. I don't want to fix people, take their pain away."

Two of the interviewees specifically mentioned wanting to offer talking-therapy alternatives to CBT, which was mentioned in terms ranging from dubious to antagonistic.

- "For me the jury's out on this one—I do know people who have found CBT really helpful, but still …"
- "I really hate CBT and what it stands for."

It seemed that many of my participants valued their way of working largely because they could offer clients the opportunity for unrestricted self-expression and the chance to be the focus of a relationship. Some respondents described this in the context of being clients themselves:

- "My therapy is the only place I express what I really feel …"
- "… the one place I am central in the relationship …"
- "… its the one chance I have to hear out loud how I am."

There was a recurring theme of participants feeling at home in both the client and therapist role. Several participants described themselves as being "the sort of people" who generally listen to and make space for others, adding that they needed to be in therapy themselves just because they were so sensitive to other peoples' needs and desires; intimate conversation was easily taken over by the priorities of their friends or family. They had people they could talk to, people they loved, but no relationship which equalled that with their psychotherapist. The most agreed-with statement in the survey (eighty-six per cent) was "Therapy gives an opportunity for a more rewarding and healing relationship than most people find in their everyday lives".

One survey respondent mentioned that she was partly inspired to train by finding the choice of black psychotherapists more limited than she would have liked—she wanted to offer something that she had found lacking herself.

### How did they come to choose psychotherapy over other possible professions?

The study gave some insight into what motivates people to pursue a psychotherapy training, apart from the hope of earning a living in an interesting and useful way. In fact, at the time they started training, the huge majority of my research participants were already established in professions that were reasonably well paid and would be commonly regarded as rewarding and/or useful. There were teachers, nurses, social workers, writers, scientists. A minority had considered other caring professions before deciding on psychotherapy, but these did not seem to centre around what they most wanted to offer. Finn said that she had looked into various types of psychology qualification and understood that they all offered better career prospects than psychotherapy, then realised that psychotherapy was what she really wanted to do.

This feeling of rightness and specialness was a recurring theme in the study:

- "It just felt right ..."
- "I couldn't bear to do anything else ..."
- "the one thing I wanted to do ..."
- "a personal journey ..."
- "the only career I can envisage keeping my interest for decades into the future ..."

The words "satisfaction", "calling", and "vocation" recurred over and over. When it came to the final section of the survey, where respondents were asked to tick one or more phrases which they felt described psychotherapy, "a vocation" got more ticks (seventy-one per cent) than "a healing profession" (sixty-six per cent) or "a helping profession" (sixty-four per cent) or "a treatment on a par with psychology or medicine" (sixty per cent). Forty per cent of respondents also described therapy as "a luxury".

## Summary of the research findings

My findings suggest that a significant proportion of people embarking on psychotherapy trainings are reluctant to consider the economics of their endeavour. Only half of the participants in my study had worked out the full cost of the fees before committing to training, even though the majority described themselves as "concerned" about the cost, and many borrowed money or made sacrifices to fund it. Even more forgot, or perhaps lacked the information, to factor in the considerable extra costs of taking part in these trainings.

Only one of my interviewees and eighteen per cent of the "Trainee" survey group said that they expected to recover the cost of their training "in the first few years" of practising. This strongly suggests to me that the hope of financial gain is only a small part of their motivation. The motivation comes from a different kind of desire: the wish to relate in a particular way to other human beings, and, in some cases, to continue and develop their own life-changing experience of being a client. The wish to "help" other people is there, but it is a particular type of help that they want to offer: not "fixing", not "removing pain", but helping another person know themselves more deeply. Psychotherapy is a vocation but also a luxury and, perhaps, given its high cost, a luxury for the giver as well as the receiver.

## Observations

I was surprised that so many of the mature professionals who took part in my study started their trainings with so little consideration of the long-term economic prospects for work, though perhaps this is a more common position than I assumed, especially for younger people now that many undergraduates get into serious debt to support their studies, with little evidence to believe their degree will easily lead to a job. The equation between getting into debt to gain qualifications and finding work is very different than it was in the days when there were more graduate-level jobs available, and fewer university entrants, and when most undergraduates had local education authority grants, and most financial institutions refused to lend to students. But many of the experienced psychotherapists in the study, including myself, took their first degrees in these conditions and still signed up for psychotherapy trainings without counting the cost.

It was interesting to look at the findings from my small study in the light of a much larger member survey carried out by the UK Council for Psychotherapy (UKCP) in 2011. Of the 1,727 UKCP survey respondents, forty-one per cent described themselves as engaged full-time in therapy-related work such as seeing clients and supervisees, teaching, and consultancy. This is a higher percentage than might be expected from looking at my results. The difference might be partly explained by the fact that the majority (sixty per cent) of the UKCP respondents had been qualified for more than ten years; there may now be a bank of well-established psychotherapists who have passed the difficult early years and are, presumably, earning a reasonable living.

Whether it will be possible for the many new psychotherapists presently in training to establish themselves in a similar way, remains to be seen. The current popularity of talking therapies in the NHS seems to be growing alongside an expectation that qualified professionals will work for very little, or nothing. At the time of writing, a private organisation called the Awareness Centre in London is bidding to take over counselling in local GP surgeries. They are advertising for volunteers, either part or fully qualified, willing to commit to seeing eight clients per week and attending group supervision, for a minimum of two years. In effect, the volunteers are expected to put in around eight hundred hours of unpaid work, far more than the number of supervised client hours required for registration. Prospective volunteers are also required to pay £150 for a training course run by the Awareness Centre. If my research participants are typical in being willing to work *pro bono* when paid work is unavailable, there may be enough psychotherapists who are willing to take on this kind of commitment. But one wonders whether these volunteers will be able to find paid work when they finish, and whether, like at least one of my research participants, they will begin to resent this stretch of unpaid work long before it is finished.

Get Stable is another organisation with an NHS counselling contract that is currently recruiting qualified therapists with experience of short-term, solution-focused work and/or CBT. Their plan is that GP surgeries will input referrals for limited-time counselling directly to Get Stable's website, and the patients concerned will be able to choose a local psychotherapist or counsellor from a list, the GP being billed at the end of each patient's course of sessions on a "no recovery, no fee" basis. The degree to which a patient has recovered will be determined by a tool on Get Stable's website in which the patient has to record their state of mind at the end of each session. Get Stable proposes paying its therapists £30 per hour, but it is hard to predict whether enough clients will deem themselves recovered in the time allowed for even this fairly modest level of pay to be sustainable.

There is also the question of how many psychotherapists from independent training institutions will be willing to work in this way.

Several participants in my study made a point of saying that they disliked CBT's focus on "fixing" problems. They were attracted to something "special" about psychotherapy that was to do with the client being listened to, developing a sense of self, creating a long-term relationship in which the client is central and can unfold in their own way and in their own time. Of course, not everyone agrees with this view that psychotherapy's value lies in extended freedom to talk; indeed, psychotherapy is sometimes criticised for keeping people "dependent" for too long, for becoming a "crutch". The NHS approach assumes that treatment for mental health problems should be as fast and efficient, and therefore as low-cost, as possible, its goal being to reduce personal distress to a manageable level. This is an understandable aim given the NHS's stretched resources, but it must be said that the short-term treatments offered by the NHS are different in kind, not just in length, from in-depth psychotherapy.

On another note, there was an aspect of my participants' enthusiasm for the experience of being a client that I found quite poignant, and this was the implication that even though these individuals valued and enjoyed their close personal relationships, they rarely had an experience outside therapy of speaking from their depths without fear of being judged, or criticised, or causing unmanageable distress, or having to listen to the other person's thoughts before they had finished expressing their own. Perhaps if we found a way to offer each other more of this in everyday life, there would be less need of psychotherapy. Perhaps a world in which psychotherapy was unnecessary would be most desirable.

I was intrigued that so many participants said that they regarded therapy as a "vocation", and in a future study it would be interesting to explore what they meant by this. The eloquence with which some of the participants spoke about psychotherapy recalled the language of religious vocation, which with some disturbing exceptions is also pursued for gains that are not primarily financial. One parallel to the psychotherapist role is the role of spiritual director in Christian communities, where the director's job is to help the directee understand and develop their relationship with God. Directors are urged to set aside their own opinions and prejudices in the service of that relationship. In psychotherapy, this translates, according to the modality, to relationship to the self, to the soul, to the body, to the world. Some people successfully combine religion/spirituality and psychotherapy, especially those in the transpersonal modalities, but perhaps for others, psychotherapy fulfils a similar need.

The sense of "feeling they had to do it whatever the cost" that many participants mentioned as a motivator for starting their trainings also recalls that of artists over the ages who accept poverty as the price of doing what they love. Nowadays, only a tiny percentage of fine art graduates make a living from selling art, but most feel privileged to spend their time creating it. In both cases, creative self-expression is seen as a "pearl of great price".

The study left me wondering whether the tendency amongst psycho-therapists to commit themselves to expensive trainings without count-ing the cost may actually affect their attitude to their clients' finances. It is a common problem that people who have undergone a particular trial themselves are reluctant to protect future generations from the same experience, even when there is good evidence that it is harmful. Consultants expect junior doctors to work the same gruelling hours as they did in their youth; parents who were smacked as children cannot see why they should not smack their own offspring: "It never did me any harm". I once went to see a psychodynamic therapist from a back-ground where several sessions a week was the norm. I was planning to see him once or perhaps twice a week; he did not pressurise me to do more, but he suggested that this would be a good idea, and I felt that he was unable to take seriously my protestations that I could not afford it. If, I argued, I came to see him four times a week, mostly in the middle of the day because he was short of early and late appointments, how could I fit in enough working hours to pay for it? And what about when I was away—at the time I had to make my holidays fit around academic terms, and usually wanted to book something before my therapist announced his holidays—and was expected to pay for four, or eight, missed sessions? The analyst countered that he too had to go through all this while he was in training, and I took this to mean that the high cost of his training was one of the things that made him feel justified in charging for missed sessions. In the end, we reached a compromise in which he gave me a reduction which may have been more than he felt he could afford, but which over time added up to more than I could.

It is certainly true that this analyst's training must have been extremely expensive, involving his being in analysis for at least four times a week over a minimum of four years. I wonder whether there is a danger that therapists, especially those qualified in high-frequency approaches, may accept too readily that such huge costs are inevitable, and unconsciously store up resentment that may later be visited on their patients, or at least cloud their perception of what a person on an average income can reasonably afford.

I have heard of therapists responding to clients' complaints about affordability by reminding them that they buy other "non-essentials"—holidays, nights out, multiple pairs of shoes—and surely their personal development and peace of mind are more important than these, so the money should be found somehow. I wonder whether such attitudes derive from sacrifices the psychotherapists made themselves during their training and early years of work, and whether the tendency that emerged in my study to treat psychotherapy as the "pearl of great price" may later cause resentment in countertransference with clients who feel differently, and who say that they cannot afford therapy. The feeling of not be able to afford it may itself be a fruitful subject for therapy—perhaps the client is experiencing the very difficulties in forming attachments that brought them to therapy in the first place, or perhaps they have a chronic difficulty in spending money on themselves. However, a client declaring a wish to end therapy because they feel they cannot afford it may be expressing an important awareness that this particular therapy, at this particular moment, with this particular therapist, is not what they need, and therefore is not a good use of money or time. The possibility that a client literally cannot—perhaps, given their circumstances, should not attempt to—find the money to pay for therapy does at least deserve some serious thought on the part of the therapist.

It is strangely hard to find in-depth discussions in the psychotherapy literature about the significance of payment between client and therapist, let alone the significance of payment between trainee and training institution. For example, existentialist psychotherapist Irvine D. Yalom (2012, p. 55) dismisses a new patient's frequent references to the cost of his therapy as "flippant", or "quips". He considers it a mark of the therapy having become serious when the references stop. He may well be right, but it is also possible that the patient has real concerns about the cost of his therapy and the likelihood or otherwise of its helping him, and that he gives up trying to discuss these concerns in the face of Yalom's refusal to engage with this subject. Similarly, psychoanalyst Patrick Casement (2006) describes the case of a patient who, whilst weaning her new baby, proposes to reduce her number of weekly sessions from four to three. Casement takes the unusual—and generous—step of offering to keep the hour available for a few weeks in case she occasionally feels the need to come for a fourth session. Casement offers this because he recognises a parallel with the baby taking the step of moving to greater independence, and wishes to support his patient during her own transition, by being available when needed. He considers his patient's request, kindly and thoughtfully, from several angles, including her fantasies around Casement's feelings about having an extra unfilled hour some weeks. The fact that cutting down her sessions in this way would save her—and cost him—money does not appear to be mentioned between them at all.

## Further questions

There were several questions I wish, with hindsight, I had included in my study, and many more that were outside the scope of my research. A little more demographic detail would have been useful in the survey. Did concerns about money vary according to gender, or marital/family status? Or was there perhaps a regional variation in practitioners' optimism about earning a good living from psychotherapy?

It would be interesting to know whether training institutions include in their syllabus any discussion of the trainees' feelings about paying for the training, and the possible knock-on effects of these feelings on their future clients. The anecdotal evidence I have heard suggests not, and perhaps training institutions could usefully consider including this subject.

I was unable to find any data about numbers of psychotherapists currently in training in the UK, how many drop out before qualifying, and how many train but never practise, although there is a rule of thumb quoted by psychotherapy trainers that one-third of graduates will practise psychotherapy full time, one-third will work part time, and one-third will never practise after qualifying. Nor could I find any statistics showing the number of people currently in psychotherapy in the UK, or what proportion of psychotherapy clients are new to therapy and what proportion also have some interest in practising it themselves. Such figures would give a fascinating insight into the economics of the psychotherapy world.

## Conclusion

The results of this small-scale investigation suggest that many people today are making major—sometimes unexamined, and perhaps unconscious—financial sacrifices to train as psychotherapists. Some are making this outlay because they see it as a sensible career move, but for many others, financial solvency and career development are not the primary motivations.

It seems that this dedication to the profession, though no doubt positive in many ways, can leave new and trainee psychotherapists potentially vulnerable to financial exploitation. Increasingly, therapy businesses contract to provide psychotherapy services to local authorities or public health organisations which are then largely staffed by volunteers who are either still in training or seeking work experience as psychotherapists. In some instances, volunteers are expected to pay for further training or for their compulsory supervision, and there is no obvious career path for many of the volunteers when their placements finish.

It would make more financial sense for new entrants to the profession to train to practise the short-term, solution-focused talking therapies that are increasingly available on the NHS, but it seems that many psychotherapists want to offer something different from this, something which could be defined as a deeper way of knowing and relating to another human being and to oneself. Enough people appear to want this to keep the profession flourishing, and if a sizeable proportion of the average psychotherapist's working life is dedicated to working with other psychotherapists, this perhaps only demonstrates how vitally important the work is to those involved in the psychotherapy world. It would seem that in our society, space for what is most deeply personal and authentic is not easily come by, except, perhaps, for those involved in some kind of spiritual or religious practice. Yet, for many of us, it is not only a luxury but an absolutely essential part of life.

## References

Casement, P. (2006). *On Learning from Life*. London: Routledge.

Entwistle, C. (2013). *Counting the Cost Study*. www.integralbody.co.uk/Resources/Counting_the_Cost_Study.pdf

UK Council for Psychotherapy (2012). *Membership Survey 2011*. London: UKCP.

Yalom, I. D. (2012). *Staring at the Sun*. Amazon Kindle Edition.

# CHAPTER NINE

# How broader research perspectives can free clients and psychotherapists to optimise their work together

*Peter Stratton*

This book is a sustained attempt to get beyond culturally accepted obviousness. An alternative image to the title of the first chapter is not of the psyche being at a crossroads but more of being stuck in the swampy lowlands (Schön, 1990) under the flyover of societal assumptions. As previous chapters have stressed, it is not just clients but also psychotherapists who can become trapped by dominant societal discourses. Perhaps in this final chapter, it is useful to go beyond reasonableness. In fact necessary, in order to promote the liberation not just of psychotherapy, but also research, to a point at which they can cooperate to offer increased benefit to everybody.

Let me propose a stance from my own background of systemic family therapy: of irreverence (Cecchin, Lane, & Ray, 1992). In proposing irreverence as a strategy for therapists' survival these authors direct us first to be irreverent to our own assumptions so that we can be freed from the taken-for-granted within our profession and our culture, and more likely to recognise our favourite beliefs not as truths but as provisional hypotheses (Cecchin would say "fantasies"). For the purposes of this chapter, I am inviting you to join me in a constructive irreverence to dominant assumptions about the relevance of research to the practice of psychotherapy.

I plan to approach this position by offering a variety of inspirations from research, going outside of the usual sources of exhortation to therapists to become more engaged with research (e.g., Stratton, 2012). This chapter explores a few of the many ways in which research can provide accessible and practical help to psychotherapists of all persuasions to shift their therapy towards greater effectiveness. But to have a chance of judging what might be useful, it would be good research guided practice to decide in advance what our question is. What is psychotherapy for?

Psychotherapy has a purpose. Can we agree that it is something about working with clients so that the functioning of their psyche is improved? Which of course can take many forms but is likely to involve changes in the ways clients experience and live their worlds and their relationships. Perhaps with increased creativity and autonomy.

Then we have a problem. If we want to be able to say anything reliable about the ways in which psychotherapy is, or may not be, fit for its purposes we must either theorise or look at what actually happens. Or both. Research has spent more than a century developing better and better ways of looking at what actually happens in ways that build a body of publically available understandings. Psychotherapy has something of a reputation for spending a century theorising. Psychotherapists also, of course, look at what actually happens in their sessions but unfortunately there is some evidence to suggest they are not totally reliable witnesses (see discussion of Kahneman, below). So this chapter is starting from a position that using research as well as theory and personal observation could be worthwhile.

But we still have a problem. Psyches are not easy to observe directly and much research has treated the psyche as a "black box". The concept of the black box[1] (Friedenberg & Silverman, 2006) describes the approach of behaviourist psychologists, notable B. F. Skinner, to sidestep the problem that the brain is too complex and unavailable to be studied directly. Stimuli enter the black box which does whatever it does, and creates responses. We can measure stimuli and responses and so can investigate the relationships between them. So psychology should build its understandings from the connections between stimuli and responses without necessarily trying to understand what connects them.

The research model that attempts to create a known psychotherapeutic stimulus and then measures the changes in symptoms that result is using this approach. Here, the black box is the psychotherapy process itself. Worse, there is a reciprocal influence. The wish to use the black box approach has driven the judgements about which research is most acceptable. So politically powerful organisations like the National Institute for Health and Social Care Excellence (NICE) have not generally been concerned to examine what goes on inside the black boxes of psychotherapy practice and the psyches of clients. They employ a hierarchy of evidence that puts randomised control trials (RCTs) at the top and qualitative research into process at the bottom of the list. This hierarchy does not include theoretical justifications or questions like "is this an obviously sensible approach to therapy?" at all. It is left to other people to develop the therapy, just as pharmaceutical companies develop psychoactive pills, and then the job of research is to compare them in terms of their consequences. The preferred methodology of an RCT is without doubt a powerful and effective approach when applied in appropriate contexts. My concern is that when applied to psychotherapy, it has been extended beyond its range of appropriateness but it is still being promoted as the "gold standard" by which all therapy research is evaluated.

I would claim that the consequences of this attempt to specify the research that is worthwhile has been damaging on many levels. It has created an image of research that many psychotherapists find unacceptable, and it has severely limited the development of other approaches. So we have a profession that is largely alienated from research, and it is not easy to offer examples of research approaches that have been developed by psychotherapists in order to deliver results that practitioners would find valuable. Such examples do exist, but they have not yet achieved a generalisable picture, and have not been priorities for funding.

## What should be the role of research?

We could start with two conventional answers: to help us understand the processes of therapy; and to advise us about what is effective. It is clear that these are not separate objectives. There is little value of knowing about a process in therapy if we have no reason to think that that process can contribute to effectiveness. And there is little value in measuring the effectiveness of a therapy if we do not know what went on in that therapy. So we need research to keep both aspects in view.

An outcome of an effective programme of research into psychotherapy is claimed to be the creation of guidelines for evidence-based practice (EBP). It is now recognised that EBP is not usefully seen as an unthinking application of directives from research evidence alone. A driving force in this movement, Sackett et al. (1996) described evidence-based medicine as:

> Evidence-based medicine is the conscientious, explicit, and judicious use of current best evidence in making decisions about the care of individual patients. The practice of evidence-based medicine means integrating individual clinical expertise with the best available external clinical evidence from systematic research. (p. 71)

Norcross et al. (2008) propose three overlapping considerations relating to: research, the client, and the clinician, with EBP decisions being the common ground shared by all three (Figure 1). This diagram suggests an onus on the therapist to ensure an adequate knowledge of the research evidence relating to the therapeutic area; a realistic appraisal of the therapist's skills, proclivities, and limitations so that they can judge which evidenced approaches they can competently and safely provide; and an understanding of the resources, life situation, and relationships of the client in order to estimate how well the evidence and the therapist's capabilities fit their needs.

Another role for research is to inform us about the Psyche and its relation to Agora, the person's context (see Chapter One). There is a wealth of research outside the field of psychotherapy that offers crucial insights into many aspects of human functioning. Not just the full range of psychological understanding across the life course, but other disciplines such as sociology, biology, and systems science. In the face of such wealth of research, we can only aspire to let our curiosity lead us out from the security of our own field into any area that looks interesting. Following trails through Wikipedia can quickly open up new vistas.

If we are unpacking the black box of the psyche, does this mean that we should now prioritise results from neuroimaging? With the publicity and substantial funding currently being given to studies of genetics and brain functioning, one might gain the impression that these are likely to open up our black box and so become the main driver of improved ways of researching psychotherapy. As a protection from

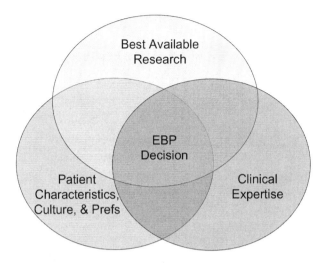

Figure 1. Mapping of the three sources of an evidence-based practice decision. After Norcross (2008). Reproduced with permission.

such reductionism, I was pleased to encounter the stance of a recent editorial in *Nature* (2013) which took a strong position about the lack of funding for research into psychological treatments for depression and the imbalance with brain research:

> The brain's complexity and relative inaccessibility leaves a gulf between the current basic understanding and the observed pathologies of human minds. Taking existing psychological therapies and improving and extending their psychological models and applications, and developing new ones, regardless of the underlying neural processes in the brain, is also a justifiable endeavour for funding agencies. Given the immediate benefits this research could bring, the deficit of interest in funding it is a scandal. (p. 474)

## What is research?

Research takes many different forms but it is possible to see all of them as leading to the creation of new understandings. There are not nuggets of objective truth waiting to be uncovered if you dig hard enough (Silverman, 1993). All research takes place in a cultural context and, at its best, contributes to the enrichment of that culture. The enrichment comes from the expansion of meanings that can be recognised and adopted within that culture. Which may in turn lead to increased capabilities. Our local research findings are unlikely to have much interest for the sentient beings of another galaxy, though they may be watching with interest as we use the products that research has made possible to render our planet uninhabitable.

So far this description of research would also cover psychotherapy. But there is more. The claim of the paragraph above entails that research will have a cultural impact. So it has become intrinsic to research that it is made public. In the process, research has developed its own elaborate culture, a central part of which is that research claims are exposed to critical review and make the public domain only if judged to meet appropriate criteria. Built into this process is an expectation that most science progresses through the steady accumulation and refinement of knowledge. Let me illustrate this with a rather disturbing claim made by Len Bickman at a meeting of CORC, the Child and Adolescent Mental Health Services (CAMHS) Outcomes Research Consortium. He pointed out that the rate of cure for childhood cancer has gone up from twenty per cent to eighty per cent in the last thirty years, while the cure rate of psychotherapy has not improved over the last forty years. (Sorry, but the rates of cure currently being reported for psychotherapy are no better than those being claimed in the 1970s.) The difference, according to Bickman, is that every child treated for cancer in the US has been part of a network of outcome studies, so every child has contributed data to our understanding of how to treat children with the condition. Almost every session of psychotherapy over the same period has contributed nothing to a knowledge base by which we can progressively improve practice.

There are both structural and cultural aspects of our field that appear to militate against a productive engagement with research. Many psychotherapists work in private practice without an institutional base that would support time spent on research. A survey of the approximately seven thousand members of the UK Council for Psychotherapy (McDonnell et al., 2012) provoked responses from five hundred and eighty-eight therapists. The factor most commonly cited to support engagement with research was working collaboratively with other therapists. Psychotherapists in the NHS might appear better placed but, in practice, research contributes little directly to the targets that have to be met, nor to prospects of job security or promotion.

Across all therapists, the greatest obstacle to research was lack of time. However, the demands of the IAPT (Improving Access to Psychological Therapies) programme for outcome data is creating something of a cultural change.

To anyone who values the contribution that research could make to the practice and profession of psychotherapy, the current limited engagement is frustrating. The overlap between the two activities means that therapists have most of the skills needed to conduct research (Stratton & Hanks, 2008). And it is easy to see a therapy as having a close correspondence with research. What is missing is the ethos that would make the understandings achieved during therapy publicly available in a form that contributes to a growing body of understanding. As a result, the immense wisdom acquired by many thousands of therapists remains the private property of each of them or, at best, is shared among a few colleagues. Accumulative research knowledge is left to career researchers and the relatively few therapist-researchers. Psychotherapists value their uniqueness and have something of a resistance to adopting standardised procedures such as manuals and outcome monitoring. But science manages to honour its maverick creative achievers while still committing to the collaborative enterprise.

There are pointers to resolving this dilemma, including Practitioner Research Networks, concepts such as the dialogical creation of multiple identities, and better understandings of universal cognitive processes that have implications for our work. These are discussed later in this chapter, but first let us consider a few areas with direct value for psychotherapists.

### Research pointers of direct value to therapists

As a warm-up, consider a few pointers that are worth thinking about, that I have understood from recent research:

- Psychotherapy has reliable positive effects in a majority of cases.
- There are very small differences in average measured effectiveness between different therapies.
- Experienced therapists draw on resources from several therapies.
- No therapist is below average in effectiveness (according to self-report by therapists).

- Clients consistently identify "being respected, being understood, and being cared for" as core elements in their experience of their therapy.
- Patient characteristics, practitioner qualities, and therapy relationship between them determine the outcome of a therapeutic process.
- Some therapists are consistently much more effective.
- One factor is belief by the therapist in the approach they are using.
- A shared belief by client and therapist may be even more powerful.
- We don't really know why *any* therapy works. In particular, we have very little understanding of when, or with whom, therapy is not useful.
- Having a siesta might lead to therapists being more attuned to positive emotions and less to negative.

As a pause for reflection, let's take that last one. Gujar et al. (2010) found that by 5 p.m. people (not therapists) who had not had a rest demonstrated heightened sensitivity to fearful and angry facial expressions. By contrast, the participants who'd had a nap were less sensitive to fearful expressions at 5 p.m. yet more sensitive to happy expressions. These emotional processing changes were also accompanied by mood differences: the no-nap group reported reduced positive mood later in the afternoon, compared with earlier, whereas the nap group reported a decrease in negative mood.

What might this rather limited piece of research get us thinking about? Should therapists have a siesta so they are more likely to feel good and alert to signs of happiness? Or should we judge when it is more appropriate to be in tune with our client's negative emotions? More broadly, such research might remind us of how sessions may be subtly influenced by the current biological state of all participants. With an idea of the range of potentially useful research, we can consider in more detail some that have brought news of difference when they were published.

For more than twenty years, Michael Lambert has been developing tools to monitor client progress in therapy and researching the effects of providing feedback to therapists. His methods have proved effective in improving outcomes (Lambert, 2007). In particular, his techniques of providing the therapist with session-by-session feedback improve overall outcome while reducing negative outcomes (Lambert et al., 2001). Lambert does not accept that clients may get worse as a precursor to getting better. Rather, his experience is that a negative trend at an early stage is predictive of treatment failure. But feeding this information back to the therapist enables them to modify their approach and significantly reduce the risk of a failed therapy (Simon et al., 2012).

The value of regular feedback to the therapist especially in cases when the therapy is not making progress has been extended by other researchers to different situations. Anker et al. (2009) report an application in couples therapy in which the feedback condition produced nearly four times the rate of clinically significant change, improvement maintained at six months, and reduced separation or divorce. This indication of the value of client-based feedback is particularly relevant given the finding by Orlinsky and Ronnestad (2005) that seventy per cent of psychotherapists treat couples. Given the limited training that most therapists have for this work, any pointers from research for improving outcomes is valuable.

Another area in which it would be good to be able to make a clear case for ways of improving therapy outcomes is the reporting of the role of "common factors". There is a widely quoted and accepted claim that the major effect within therapy is provided by the factors common to all psychotherapies, with treatment modality a much weaker contributor. Given that the precise percentages offered (though not here, for good reason) were introduced without a valid empirical basis one must wonder why the enthusiastic acceptance. One positive interpretation is that the claim liberates us from what have become called the culture wars in psychotherapy. Perhaps we are growing away from strident claims about which modality of therapy is best. Perhaps we refuse to be corralled by the attempts by NICE to find one therapy that is better than any other for each diagnosed condition. There is no shortage of research to support the claim of little difference on average between therapies. For example, Cuijpers et al. (2008) report meta-analyses of research into seven different therapies for depression (cognitive behaviour therapy (CBT), non-directive supportive treatment, behavioural activation treatment, psychodynamic treatment, problem-solving therapy, interpersonal psychotherapy (IPT), and social skills training). They concluded that there was no substantial indication that any of the treatments was more or less efficacious though IT was a little stronger, and CBT had a higher drop-out rate. Their conclusion that different interventions have comparable benefits was confirmed by a subsequent, more extensive review (Barth et al., 2013).

Within common factors, it is the alliance between therapist and client that has emerged with the most consistent claim. The collection edited by John Norcross (2011) under the title of *Psychotherapy Relationships that Work* is a powerful statement of this position and ends up offering very concrete ways of converting the research into improved practice. Friedlander et al. (2006) offer a detailed guide to making therapeutic alliances work in couple and in family therapy. Their research generated four dimensions of the therapeutic alliance:

- engagement in the therapeutic process,
- emotional connection to the therapist,
- safety within the therapeutic system,
- shared sense of purpose within the family.

Finally, a remarkable example of the value of looking for the wider consequences of psychotherapy comes under the heading of "medical offset". Crane and Christenson (2008) analysed data on the families who had been high utilisers of medical services. Those who participated in a brief marital and family therapy showed significant reductions of sixty-eight per cent for health screening visits, thirty-eight per cent for illness visits, fifty-six per cent for laboratory/X-ray visits, and seventy-eight per cent for urgent care visits. Some of the benefits were stronger for family members than they were for the referred client. It is good to know that therapy can have such general value. It is also good to have this kind of research data when trying to convince politicians of the financial benefits of supporting psychotherapy provision.

## Some other directions we might find it useful to explore

If we want to take a fresh look at ways in which research could be useful to psychotherapy it may help to start from some perspectives that have come from elsewhere.

### Fast and slow thinking

In 1901, Freud published *The Psychopathology of Everyday Life*. This book has had an extraordinary impact over more than a century and was based on his interpretations of his careful empirical observations.

Much of its value came from the universal relevance of its application of Freud's methods and concepts. I would suggest that the modern equivalent is Daniel Kahneman's *Thinking, Fast and Slow* (2011). This book is an invaluable collation of research findings about common tendencies in human thinking that often misdirect our understandings. It can not only give insights into how clients think, but maybe more importantly about how therapists think. For example, therapists live a very significant part of their lives in therapy sessions. We are thereby likely to place undue emphasis on the significance for clients of their experiences in the session. As Kahneman (2011, p. 402) points out, "nothing is as important as it seems to be while you are thinking about it". And he devotes a whole chapter to the many factors that lead us to be sure we are right despite having no good basis for that certainty. He thinks it particularly likely that psychotherapists will lack feedback about long-term consequences. But because our intuition usually works well, we "… have not learned to identify the situations and the tasks in which intuition will betray them. The unrecognised limits of professional skill help explain why experts are often overconfident" (p. 242).

The difference from Freud is that Kahneman has available a century of empirical research which he coordinates into a wide ranging set of insights into the foibles of human thinking. Though strangely, he does not reference Freud. Perhaps most pertinent is his underlying theory in which he separates thinking into the *fast*, intuitive unexamined, practical understanding by which we live our everyday lives and the effort-ful, *slow*, considered process by which we can exert a degree of control over fast thinking, when we recognise that we need to do so. Perhaps there is a real difference between psychotherapy modalities in the balance they offer between fast and slow. Working with several families simultaneously (multifamily therapy, Asen & Scholz, 2010) must demand much more intuitive thinking and responding than a series of psychoanalytic sessions in which the onus is on the therapist to ponder deeply before offering an intervention. But Kahneman is very clear: it is not that one kind of thinking makes mistakes and the other reliably gets things right. Both systems readily result in errors, but the errors are of different kinds. It may seem onerous to propose that all therapists should read the 418 pages of this text but as an example of the power of coordinated research insights to tell us how our psyche is working, it is quite exceptional.

*Therapist identity*

Therapists do not come in a standardised form, however intensive the training and however rigorous the manual they are following. Heinonen et al. (2102) report that active, engaging, and extroverted therapists produced faster symptom reduction in short-term therapy than in long-term therapy. But more cautious, non-intrusive therapists generated greater benefits in long-term therapy. I would incline to caution about classifying therapists by personality type when so much work is being done to escape from the idea that we each have a stable, fixed identity.

One set of concepts that may help to connect to the effects of forming a new and changing alliance with each client comes from the dialogical construction of identities. This body of theory takes the position that new identities are constructed in every dialogical encounter. So we can think of a therapy session as rehearsing new possibilities and variations of identity which, once experienced, might be more readily available in other future dialogues. The theory of dialogical construction of identities was formulated by Hermans & DiMaggio (2004) following Bakhtin (1973) in the context of research into child development. Valsiner (2002) stresses the dynamic functioning of the dialogical self as the way that people create meaning in their relationships. I would suggest that a therapist will have created several thousand identities during their work. Now we can make another link. We guide our lives through anticipations (the basic tenet of George Kelly's personal construct therapy, 1955) and especially our expectations about the consequences of our actions (Stratton, 2003). If we add formation of the identities of client and therapist that are dialogically constructed during the therapy, then we have a basis for theorising the importance of shared expectations of the effects of the therapy that research has found to be so important.

People live their lives in a complex web of relationships. A psychotherapist enters the client's web at a particular time and general system theory will point out that creating this new relationship will provide some kind of perturbation for all of their other relationships (Hills, 2013). But equally, changes in those relationships, whether or not related to the therapy, will impinge on the interactions with their therapist.

## How therapy works

For researching into longer-term consequences to be useful, we need to relate them to appropriate scale processes during therapy. But what is an appropriate scale? The discussion above suggests the relevant aspects may occur in microseconds, or over many hours. So how do we tackle this? If the research showing that differences between therapists are larger than differences between modalities, one route would be to find the consistently effective therapists and see in what ways they differ from averagely effective therapists.

Catastrophe theory claims that small, maybe even arbitrary events can be the occasion for dramatic and irreversible change. But the change is unpredictable so we have to be prepared for therapy to have such effects. How much of our current theorising and recommendations for practice is a doomed attempt to specify in advance the effects we will have? Psychotherapy is a small part of most people's lives. But it can be a tipping point into substantial, irreversible and unpredicted change. So there are two kinds of therapeutic process to research. The steady accumulation of the constant trusting therapeutic relationship conducive to the goals of the therapy, and the immediate precursors to significant moments.

Tipping points are made likely by the slow accumulation of good therapeutic interactions. So research that attempts to identify the specific events without embedding them in the context of evolving therapeutic transactional adaptations will not be informative. The momentary events themselves would be a misleading guide to therapists about what they should try to achieve. We could find ways to identify significant moments and then study them in relation to the surrounding therapeutic processes to see if we can gain a better understanding of whether they happen, why they happen and, if their importance is verified, how we can help clients, therapists and trainers to optimise them.

There is evidence that many experienced therapists operate a repertoire of competences that they can draw on to meet the needs of each session. Recently this has emerged as an issue of integrating different modalities with an idea that drawing on aspects outside of the theoretical context that gives them meaning can be ineffectual or worse. Norcross and Beutler (2011) have published an overview in which they usefully distinguish: technical eclecticism, theoretical integration;

common factors; and assimilative integration. They then proceed to demonstrate the value of systematic integration and show that it is a dominant approach at least in the United States. They conclude that "Integrative psychotherapies are intellectually vibrant, clinically popular, and demonstrably effective" (p. 531). More specifically, Breunlin et al. (2011) are proposing an "integrative problem-centred metaframeworks therapy" (IPCM).

## Conclusion

Psychotherapists may find themselves being offered a mixture of exhortation and practical advice about ways of gaining benefit from engaging with research. There is even a literature on possible obstructions ranging from the survey by McDonnell et al. (2012) to a detailed proposal for training research-informed clinicians. Karam and Sprenkle (2010) see much of the problem deriving from the Boulder Scientist-Practitioner Model. This model was adopted by clinical psychology and has been presented as an aspiration for all psychotherapy. It may well be that it has resulted in the expectations being set unrealistically high, such that most practising psychotherapists have wisely decided that what is on offer in psychotherapy research is not worth the limited gain.

This chapter has attempted to take a wider perspective than the usual focus on politically expedient uses of research through quantitative outcome measurement or qualitative analysis of process. Our clients' psyches inhabit a modern world in which research is readily available in the media and on the internet, and we all use it freely in making decisions in our lives. They might be surprised to find that much of psychotherapy proceeds without much reference to research and increasingly, we are finding that potential clients have tried to research us on the Web before deciding whether to try forming a therapeutic alliance with us. Hopefully there are some tantalising clues in this chapter to suggest that there will be a form of research somewhere that could satisfy the curiosity that earlier chapters of this book have created for you.

Williams et al. (2006) liken the clinician's use of research to panning for gold. I would, of course, want to argue that the gold takes the form of enhanced understanding, but let them have the last word:

> Eventually, most clinicians can overcome the challenges inherent in using research to inform clinical practice. ... Research has the

potential to improve client services if it supplements (but does not replace) a clinician's wisdom and judgment. Indeed, we believe that the field as a whole will benefit if a critical mass of clinicians are willing to examine how their practice is both supported and challenged by the research. These benefits, we believe, are worth their weight in gold. (p. 29)

## Acknowledgements

I am grateful to Helga Hanks and members of the UKCP Research Faculty Committee: Angela Cotter, Tirril Harris, Andrew Wadge, and Nick Midgley for ideas and helpful critiques of earlier versions of this chapter.

## Note

1. Note that the use of "black box" for the recorders in aircraft is misleading in two ways. First, the whole point is to be able to find out what is inside them. Second, they are coloured orange.

## References

Anker, M. G., Duncan, B. L., & Sparks, J. A. (2009). Using client feedback to improve couple therapy outcomes: a randomized clinical trial in a naturalistic setting. *Journal of Consulting and Clinical Psychology, 77(4)*: 693–704.

Asen, E., & Scholz, M. (2010). *Multi-Family Therapy: Concepts and Techniques.* London: Routlege.

Bakhtin, M. (1973). *Problems of Dostoevsky's Poetics* (2nd edn.; Trans. R. W. Rotsel). Ann Arbor, MI: Ardis. (Original work published 1929 as *Problemy tvorchestva Dostoevskogo* [Problems of Dostoevsky's Art]).

Barth, J., Munder, T., Gerger, H., Nüesch, E., & Trelle, S. (2013). Comparative efficacy of seven psychotherapeutic interventions for patients with depression: a network meta-analysis. PLOS Medicine, 10(5): e1001454. doi:10.1371/journal.pmed.1001454.

Breunlin, D. C., Pinsof, W. M., Russell, W. P., & Lebow, J. (2011). Integrative problem-centered metaframeworks (IPCM) therapy; 1: Core concepts and hypothesizing. *Family Process, 50*: 293–313.

Cecchin, G., Lane, G., & Ray, W. (1992). *Irreverence: A Strategy for Therapist Survival.* London: Karnac.

Crane, D. E., & Christenson, J. D. (2008). The medical offset effect: patterns in outpatient services reduction for high utilizers of health care. *Contemporary Family Therapy, 30*: 127–138.

Cuijpers, P., van Straten, A., Andersson, G., & van Oppen, P. (2008). Psychotherapy for depression in adults: a meta-analysis of comparative outcome studies. *Journal of Consulting and Clinical Psychology, 76*: 909–922.

Freud, S. (1901b). *The Psychopathology of Everyday Life. SE., 6*: 1–279. London: Hogarth.

Friedenberg, J., & Silverman, G. (2006). *Cognitive Science: An Introduction to the Study of Mind*. London: Sage.

Friedlander, M. L., Escudero, V., & Heatherington, L. (2006). *Therapeutic Alliances in Couple and Family Therapy: An Empirically Informed Guide to Practice*. New York: APA Books.

Gujar, N., McDonald, S., Nishida, M., & Walker, M. (2010). A role for REM sleep in recalibrating the sensitivity of the human brain to specific emotions. *Cerebral Cortex, 21(1)*: 115–123.

Heinonen, E., Lindfors, O., Laaksonen, M. A., & Knekt, P. (2012). Therapists' professional and personal characteristics as predictors of outcome in short- and long-term psychotherapy. *Journal of Affective Disorders, 138(3)*: 301–312.

Hermans, H. J. M., & Dimaggio, G. (Eds.) (2004). *The Dialogical Self in Psychotherapy*. London: Brunner-Routledge.

Hills, J. (2013). *Introduction to Systemic and Family Therapy*. Basingstoke: Palgrave Macmillan.

Kahneman, D. (2011). *Thinking, Fast and Slow*. London: Allen Lane.

Karam, E. A., & Sprenkle, D. H. (2010). The research-informed clinician: a guide to training the next-generation MFT. *Journal of Marital and Family Therapy, 36*: 307–319.

Kelly, G. (1955). *A Theory of Personality*. New York: Norton.

Lambert, M. (2007). Presidential address: what we have learned from a decade of research aimed at improving psychotherapy outcome in routine care. *Psychotherapy Research, 17(1)*: 1–14.

Lambert, M. J., Whipple, J. L., Smart, D. W., Vermeersch, D. A., Nielsen, S. L., & Hawkins, E. J. (2001). The effects of providing therapists with feedback on patient progress during psychotherapy: are outcomes enhanced? *Psychotherapy Research, 11(1)*: 49–68.

McDonnell, L., Stratton, P., Butler, S., & Cape, N. (2012). Developing research-informed practitioners—an organisational perspective. *Counselling and Psychotherapy Research: Linking Research with Practice, 12*: 167–177.

Nature Editorial (2013). Therapy deficit. *Nature, 489(7471)*: 473–474.

Norcross, J. C. (2011). *Psychotherapy Relationships that Work* (2nd edn.). New York: Oxford University Press.

Norcross, J. C., & Beutler, L. E. (2011). Integrative psychotherapies. In: R. J. Corsini & D. Wedding (Eds.), *Current Psychotherapies* (9th edn.). Belmont, CA: Brooks/Cole Cengage.

Norcross, J. C., Hogan, T. P., & Koocher, G. P. (2008). *Clinician's Guide to Evidence-Based Practices: Mental Health and the Addictions*. New York: Oxford University Press.

Orlinsky, D. E., & Ronnestad, M. H. (2005). *How Psychologists Develop: A Study of Therapeutic Work and Professional Growth*. Washington, DC: American Psychological Association.

Sackett, D. L., Rosenberg, W. M. C., Gray, J. A. M., Haynes, R. B., & Richardson, W. S. (1996). Evidence-based medicine: what it is and what it isn't. *British Medical Journal, 312*: 71–72.

Schön, D. A. (1990). *Educating the Reflective Practitioner: Towards a New Design for Teaching and Learning*. San Francisco: Jossey Bass.

Silverman, D. (1993). *Interpreting Qualitative Data: Methods for Analysing Text, Talk and Interaction*. London: Sage.

Simon, W., Lambert, M. J., Harris, M. W., Busath, G., & Vazquez, A. (2012). Providing patient progress information and clinical support tools to therapists: effects on patients at risk of treatment failure. *Psychotherapy Research, 22(6)*: 638–647.

Stratton, P. (2003). How families and therapists construct meaning through anticipatory schemas. *Human Systems, 14*: 119–130.

Stratton, P. (2007a). Dialogical construction of the selves of trainees as competent researchers. *Journal of Family Therapy, 29*: 342–345.

Stratton, P. (2007b). Systemic and research contributions to happiness in families. *Human Systems, 18*: 126–134.

Stratton, P. (2012). Realistic relationships between psychotherapy and research: implications for training and practice. *The Psychotherapist, 51*: 6–8.

Stratton, P., & Hanks, H. (2008). From therapeutic skills to research competence: making use of common ground. *Human Systems, 19*: 153–171.

Valsiner, J. (2002). Forms of dialogical relations and semiotic autoregulation within the self. *Theory and Psychology, 12(2)*: 251–265.

Williams, L. M., Patterson, J. E., & Miller, R. B. (2006). Panning for gold: a clinician's guide to using research. *Journal of Marital and Family Therapy, 29*: 407–426.

# INDEX